THE
THERAPEUTIC
INTERACTION

A SYNTHESIS

THE THERAPEUTIC INTERACTION

A SYNTHESIS

ROBERT LANGS, M.D.
Clinical Assistant Professor of Psychiatry
State University of New York
Downstate Medical Center

JASON ARONSON, INC.
New York, New York

Langs, Robert J.
　The therapeutic interaction

　Bibliography
　Includes index.
　1. Psychotherapist　and　patient.　I. Title.
RC480.5L36　　　　　　　616.8'914

ISBN: 0-87668-329-4

Library of Congress Catalog Number: 77-84414

Manufactured in the United States of America

to
Joan and Jack,
Harold,
Lynn and David,
Bonny and Edward.

Classical Psychonalysis and Its Applications:

A Series of Books Edited by Robert Langs, M.D.

ARONSON

Contents

Chapter 3   49

THE PATIENT'S RELATIONSHIP TO THE ANALYST

Preface

This book is a revised reproduction of Part 6 of Volume
II of *The Therapeutic Interaction*. As such, it represents an
effort to delineate in a highly condensed fashion the
essential components and dimensions of the psychotherapeutic and psychoanalytic relationships and interactions.
While it is, indeed, a personal crystallization, its main
ingredients are drawn only in part from my clinical
experience; a major source is the psychoanalytic literature
abstracted and discussed in earlier sections of *The
Therapeutic Interaction.* It is my hope that this synthesis will
help the reader sort out the many complexities of the
therapeutic relationship and process, and that it will
encourage new clinical questions and studies, prompt a
renewed or continuing interest in the literature on which
this work is based, and lead to improved understanding
and therapeutic techniques. These goals ask a great deal of
the reader, but then, so does the therapeutic interaction
itself.

Robert Langs, M.D.
New York, New York

THE THERAPEUTIC INTERACTION

A SYNTHESIS

Chapter 1

Psychotherapy, Psychoanalysis and the Validating Process

The intricacies of the dyadic relationship between the patient and his analyst or therapist stagger the imagination. No attempt at synthesis can be entirely satisfactory or complete: all I can hope to do is provide a skeleton that incorporates its various elements, leaving the reader to flesh out the structure with his own sensitivities and appreciation of its attributes.

Inevitably, I must sketch with a broad pen: while the implications for technique are here, I shall not specially explore many of the technical ramifications of what I have to say. For those who quite rightly demand—as I myself have always expected—clinical documentation of psychoanalytic hypotheses, I have recently published *The Bipersonal Field* (Langs, 1976a). That work functions as a companion piece to the present volume, documenting in detail the broad ideas outlined here. In the present writing, I shall concentrate on clinical hypotheses and formulations, without diversion into specific clinical material or reiteration of the references on which a particular concept is based. The latter I have documented in the two volumes of *The Therapeutic Interaction* (1976b), and, though for purposes of exposition and clarity they will not be retraced, I fully acknowledge my indebtedness.

Psychoanalysis and Psychotherapy: A Comparison

In this synthesis, my model will be the psychoanalytic situation, although I believe most of the basic considerations apply with essentially equal validity to the psychotherapeutic setting as well. I am well aware that this is a much debated issue, and I shall try here, without polemics, to indicate specific differences between the two where they are present and relevant. However, to make this synthesis applicable to both psychotherapy and psychoanalysis, I shall first attempt a brief clarification of the similarities and differences between these two therapeutic modalities.

The psychoanalytic and psychotherapeutic situations are both founded on a bipersonal field created through a structured relationship between patient and healer. They differ essentially in only two main operational variables: the frequency of the sessions and the position of the patient vis-à-vis the analyst or therapist. The patient's investment in the relationship is no less in psychotherapy than in psychoanalysis. Analysts, I believe, have in general made many assumptions about psychotherapy, as distinguished from psychoanalysis, that are based less on validated precepts than on their own inappropriate needs for a treatment modality in which the persistently frustrating renunciations so essential to analysis could be modified. If we allow clinical observations to prevail over theoretical or countertransference-based biases, our conclusions will point to many areas of similarity between the two situations, as well as to a number of significant differences.

It is important at the outset not to underestimate the constructive intrapsychic modifications that can be achieved through analysis and adaptive structural change, and to recognize that less intensive psychotherapy cannot as a rule produce a comparable outcome; on the other hand, it is equally important not to underestimate the potential for structural change that can be derived from sound work within the latter situation. The analytic experience, however, provides for greater opportunities for insight, extensive genetic reconstructions, analysis of pathogenic unconscious fantasies, memories, and introjects, and for an especially intense interaction with a managing and interpreting analyst with whom, it is to be hoped, continual, positive introjective identifications can be effected. As a result it offers, through a therapeutic interaction, the most extensive and lasting means currently available of generating positive intrapsychic changes. In general, the psychotherapeutic experience, when properly handled, offers an opportunity for a limited and modified version of these processes and inner changes.

Thus, the differences in the two treatment forms appear to be quantitative rather than qualitative. The same basic bilateral needs and goals prevail in both situations, and in both there is a potentially curative interaction within which certain fundamental processes are crucial; for both, too, this interaction and the offer of valid interpretations are the central curative experiences and factors (see Langs, 1973, 1974, 1975a, b, c, 1976a for clinical evidence and documentation).

I would suggest that both the psychoanalytic and psychotherapeutic situations call for the establishment of a well-defined framework as the substructure of the necessary therapeutic situation, and that this frame is quite comparable in the two therapeutic settings. (For example, some therapists use the couch with patients seen one to three times weekly—a practice that needs more intensive investigation.) Clinical observation has failed to justify the tendency among psychoanalysts either to neglect or to modify quite readily the framework of the psychotherapeutic situation; indeed, these practices appear fraught with all the consequences of unnecessary deviations in analytic technique and other technical errors. The framework, it is clear, represents a basic therapeutic hold and need, essential in establishing the unique properties of any therapeutic relationship, and in offering the patient a secure situation and a field of interaction with healing potential.

A second area of confusion concerning the distinction between therapy and analysis has to do with the long-standing question of the availability and analyzability of the derivatives of unconscious transference fantasies. A related issue involves the extent of the patient's unconscious sensitivities, especially his unconscious perceptions of, and introjective identifications with, the therapist or analyst. Pertinent to this is the extent to which projective and introjective mechanisms prevail in the therapeutic and analytic interactions, and thus the broader question of the importance of the interactional components in the two therapeutic modalities. We might also ask how a number of complex processes are affected, if at all, by the choice of treatment form, and include here the extent of regression, the depth of treatment, the availability of derivatives of early childhood experiences, and the presence of analyzable expressions of primitive and other pathogenic memories, introjects, and core unconscious fantasies.

To answer briefly, degree of regression and depth of treatment seem functions of a number of factors. The most prominent are: the therapeutic framework, including frequency of visits, positioning of the participants, and all the other ground rules and boundaries; the patient's psychopathology, including the deformities of his character structure, defenses, instinctual drives, superego—ego ideal system, self-system and image, and the like; his specific self-representations, the history of his early relationships, and his current capacity for object relatedness, trust, reality testing, creative synthesis, integration, and other relatively autonomous ego functioning. With respect to the analyst or therapist, the nature of his hold and capacity to create a proper, adaptively changeable therapeutic climate should be considered, as well as his personality, character structure, structural balances, genetic history, intrapsychic conflicts, relatively autonomous ego functioning, style of working, and other basic attributes. Other factors include the nature of the specific therapeutic alliance and its vicissitudes, the details of the ongoing therapeutic interaction, and the particular internal and external reality events that occur for each participant in the course of treatment. In the face of such complex determinants, facile statements regarding the comparative experience of a patient in therapy or analysis are of little value.

We may note, however, some broad trends. In general, more frequent sessions and use of the couch tend to produce greater regression, to make available deeper derivatives of core unconscious fantasies, memories, and introjects, and to render accessible for more intensive study a wider range of unconscious transference fantasies and interactions. In addition, the analytic framework generates a relatively greater sense of intensity, intimacy, potential for feelings of fusion, and quality of caring than is seen in therapy, and the boundaries between the two participants have a greater tendency to blur. Use of the couch diminishes the reality stimuli available to the patient, and the respective positions of the patient and analyst provide an impetus for sexual, submissive, and aggressive fantasies. The setting influences the patient's nontranference and transference responses, as well as the communications of analyzable derivatives in the cognitive-verbal and interactional-nonverbal spheres. Intrapsychic defenses are more likely to be in evidence and available for modification of both their adaptive and maladaptive functions and the unconscious fantasies they express and are based on. In analysis, the patient's conscious and unconscious perceptions of and reactions to the analyst are both more sensitive and more likely to be distorted than is the case in therapy. On the whole, in the analytic situation, the transference component is also more pervasive, more extensively communicated in its diverse expressions, and more primitive. Interactionally, the patient is intensely involved with his analyst, who becomes an overridingly important object for him.

Comparable trends, albeit in far more attenuated forms, are found in the analyst. He tends to experience a more intimate therapeutic hold and a greater thrust toward fusion with the patient than does the psychotherapist. His own inappropriate needs to make use of the patient for holding and containing functions are heightened, and his sexual, dominating, and aggressive unconscious fantasies are intesified—all pressures that may prompt counter-transference responses. On the other hand, mastery of them contributes to a positive therapeutic atmosphere and to the analyst's professional adequacy. While counter-transference manifestations may therefore be more intense in analysis (though it is difficult to generalize because of the many variables), the analyst's special intimacy with his patient enables his comprehension, sensitivities, and empathic reactions to interpenetrate his work more effectively than in therapy, affording him a greater capacity to interpret and respond therapeutically to his patient, and a wider opportunity for insight and inner adaptive change for himself—even though that is, of course, not a primary function of the analytic situation.

The analytic setting, then, creates an intense relationship with great pressures toward dependency and emotional closeness, instinctual-drive expressions, the mobilization of pathological introjects, and reactive defenses. Interactionally, it presents both participants extensive opportunities for projective and introjective identifications,* for bilateral therapeutic regression, and for potential misalliances.

The patient in psychotherapy, on the other hand, despite the relative diminution of the factors described above, nonetheless develops an intense investment in his relationship with his therapist. Strong transference and nontransference responses are just as central to his adaptational efforts as they are for the analysand, and they also become pertinent to maladaptations related to his symptoms and characterological disturbances. The therapist who wishes to offer the patient an opportunity for inner structural change has, therefore, no choice but to do much of the therapeutic work in this area. The exploration and working through of external relationships and traumas—which also take place in analysis—are in general secondary, though valuable, in both modalities. The expressions of the transference components in therapy, through both the patient's associations and his interaction

---

* *Projective Identification: An actual interactional effort to psychologically place into another person aspects of one's inner state (see chapter 5).*

Introjective Identification: The psychological, interactional unconscious incorporation of some aspect of the inner state of another person (see chapter 5).

with the therapist, will tend to be less intense and less regressed than in analysis, but analytic exploration and working through are feasible—and essential—to therapeutic outcome. Where severe psychopathology is present in the patient, and when the therapist introduces major countertransference-based disturbances, psychotherapy will disclose more primitive derivatives, although they generally will not be as extensively explored and resolved as in analysis. Interactionally, the same basic mechanisms prevail in the two therapeutic situations, although to different degrees. Efforts at projective and introjective identification can be documented in both psychotherapy patients and their psychotherapists, although the ramifications tend not to be as extensively understood and worked through as in analysis.

The face-to-face mode introduces a less global therapeutic hold for the patient, a less amorphous and primitve sense of hold for the therapist, and a less pervasive sense of intimacy for both participants than is available in the analytic relationship. It brings to the relationship a greater sense of reality: visual cues—for example, facial expressions and body movements—are available to the patient and diminish, but by no means exclude, his experience and communication of distortions in his perceptions of the therapist. This situation also offers clearer physical-spatial boundaries to the therapeutic relationship, and may lessen the extent to which both patient and therapist become caught up in their inner fantasies. It provides both participants with sharper reminders of the realities of the therapeutic relationship, and their influence on the distorted and nondistorted components. For both, it may generate problems about being seen and intensify exhibitionistic-voyeuristic anxieties, although these may also occur, in a different form, in the analytic situation.

In all, both psychotherapy and psychoanalysis require a basic framework, and reflect fundamentally similar mechanisms and qualities. Issues such as whether the patient in psychotherapy develops a transference neurosis or whether it is feasible to "analyze the transference" in this setting seem to fade into the background and become matters of relative proportion; the creation of a therapeutic bipersonal field and the need to do the therapeutic work along the interface created by the patient and his therapist or analyst comes to the fore. From this perspective, the similarity of the fundamentals of the two situations may be recognized, the extensive potential influences on the specific nature of a given therapeutic or analytic experience taken into account, and the generally undeniable greater effectiveness of the analytic situation empirically established.

In the synthesis that follows, I shall not further attempt a special differentiation of the relative qualities of any given aspect of the therapeutic relationship in psychotherapy and psychoanalysis. In the main, I will be alluding to the analytic situation, and will qualify my comments only where absolutely necessary. However, before turning to the synthesis itself, I wish to outline the methodology on which it is based. With this in mind, I turn to the problem of validation.

The Validating Process

The patient-analyst relationship begins and unfolds as an interaction, initiated with a specific goal and created within a definitive psychophysical setting—a bipersonal field. It is a complex, continuing, patterned interchange of stimulus and response, search and defense, movement

toward and away from, revelation and concealment—
among many other dimensions. It is a situation of such
extensive conscious and unconscious mutual influence
that any particular moment or any special dimension of the
relationship can be comprehended only by taking into
account all components of the field, including the
behaviors and inner state of each participant. Efforts to
isolate one or another segment of this interaction require
repeated allusions to other areas; such a separation is at
best a heuristic device for concentrating on a given
element, and is inevitably incomplete.

Before attempting such a dissection and reintegration,
there is one operation that must be defined and applied,
explicitly or otherwise, by any observer or participant who
wishes to comprehend what occurs within this interaction.
In analysis or therapy, surface behavior, manifest events,
and apparent content of communications are only one (and
often an unreliable) level of interaction and possible
understanding. If we are to investigate and conceptualize
these therapeutic situations, we must establish a psychoanalytic methodology through which experiences within
this interactional field can be identified and verified, and
statements about these events given full and accurate
meaning on all possible levels—manifest and latent, conscious and unconscious.

There is a general sequence of therapeutic events in the
analytic situation. If we look at this in model form it takes
on the following appearance: communication (usually by
the patient, more rarely by the analyst), formulation and
intervention (usually by the analyst, more rarely by the
patient), and response (in the usual situation, primarily
within the patient and secondarily within the analyst,
although the reverse may also occur). While considerable
importance may be accorded each of these steps, my stress

here is on the third phase, that of confirmation or nonconfirmation, since it is here that the validation of the entire sequence takes place; this is the means through which we give credence to the relevance of a given formulation for the microcosm of the particular patient-analyst relationship and for the macrocosm of psychoanalytic theory. Since it will not be feasible, in presenting my synthesis of the patient-analyst relationship, to repeatedly discuss issues of validation and to review the status of each idea in this regard, I shall here examine the essential elements of validation so that they may be accepted as implicit in my entire presentation.

The Validating Process within the Analyst. Among the therapeutic responsibilities of the analyst is his task of comprehending the communications of the patient—behavioral and verbal—in order to formulate their implications, offer interventions and especially interpretations to the patient, and, finally, assess both the analysand's and his own responses to these interventions. The therapeutic measures taken by the analyst include not only his verbal comments, but also his management of the framework; the validating process must be applied to his efforts in both spheres.

The relatively infrequent considerations of validation as it applies to the analytic relationship have focused on the analyst's verbal interventions and the means through which he assesses their accuracy and therapeutic effects by evaluating in depth the patient's subsequent associations and other responses. If we take this as our initial model, we may note in general that the analyst strives to understand the patient's symptoms and their underlying basis, in terms of the specific dynamics of the moment as they relate to his past. He looks especially at the continuing interaction between himself and the patient, the nature of the patient's associations, and the immediate sources of the patient's anxiety or other inner disturbance—his primary adaptive tasks within and without the therapeutic relationship.

Using a variety of inner and outer inputs, the analyst establishes the central adaptive context for the patient's communications and endeavors, and attends freely to the unconscious meanings of both the analysand's verbal associations and his nonverbal, implicit communications. He alternates between, on the one hand, these unbiased receptive processes and, on the other, efforts to make connections with past communications and to recognize meaningful patterns in the patient's present associations. As he formulates and synthesizes, decomposes and reintegrates, the analyst generally attempts to generate and confirm a series of *silent hypotheses,* while maintaining his further openness and receptiveness.

Schematically, from the vantage point of the analyst, we may consider these private efforts at validation, which are based on an evaluation of the patient's continuing associations and past material, as well as on a cognitive-affective inner assessment derived from the analyst's subjective feelings and associations, his recall of prior material from the patient, and his sense of "fit" or explanatory power, as the first point of validation by the analyst in the psychoanalytic process. This first effort at confirmation may show considerable fluctuation, may call for repeated reformulation, and, ideally, will eventually coalesce around a budding interpretation that takes into account both the prior associations from the patient and the series of associations that follow the silent crystallization of the particular formulation.

As a rule, it is only when a silent hypothesis has been validated in the basic spheres of the patient's ongoing associations, of the analyst's cognitive assessment of the prior and present material, and of his own subjective feeling of correctness and pertinence (here, less rational or more global processes may participate in addition to secondary process, logical, reality-oriented, evaluative thinking) that the analyst, at a well-chosen moment, will offer an intervention to the patient. At this juncture a second point of validation is at hand.

In outlining the components of this next step in the validating process, let us be reminded that while verbal communications, and especially the analyst's interpretations, are generally recognized as the focal point, there are two other types of intervention that call for definitive confirmation: (1) the handling of a specific issue or any active undertaking related to the management of the framework, and (2) prolonged silences on the part of the analyst—his not intervening. In general, the definitive phase of the validating process consists of the analyst's scrutiny of his subjective awareness and of the patient's communications. The main elements of this process are:
1. The immediate subjective reactions—affects and thoughts—of the anlyst himself: (a) his cognitive assessment of the actual intervention—his afterthoughts— based on a review of the material on which the intervention was based and on a further consideration of the prior material from and behaviors of the patient, and of earlier interventions and subjective responses in the analyst; (b) his ongoing controlled or uncontrolled associations, verbal or imagistic, including the emergence of conscious fantasies; (c) his immediate conscious and unconscious

perceptions and assessment of the patient's initial response; (d) his immediate, unconscious or conscious introjective identification with the patient's reactions, and his conscious and unconscious processing of this identificatory occurrence; (e) his initial empathic and intuitive responses to the patient's reactions to the intervention, and his intuitive and less clearly rational assessment of his own intervention; (f) his evaluation and integration of these experiences.

2. The pursuit, over time, of these responses and assessments, and in addition, a special focus on the patient's subsequent associations and behaviors for indications of confirmation or its absence.

Once the analyst has intervened through an interpretation, prolonged silence, or management of the relationship and its frame, his communication to the patient becomes a primary adaptive context for comprehending the subsequent associations and behaviors of the analysand. The analyst's cognitive abilities continue to be supplemented by his empathy and intuition; by his controlled and momentary introjective identifications with the various processes, introjects, contents, and structures within the patient; by his experiences as the patient's object and his identification with the inner objects of the analysand; and by his processing of the patient's projective identifications—the contents and evocations of proxy that are interactionally communicated by the patient and placed into the analyst. Efforts at validation by the analyst, then, rely on his cognitive capacities and other secondary process-dominated, relatively autonomous ego functions; more primary process-dominated fantasies, intuitions, empathic responses, and the like; and his inner processing of the interaction with the patient—the contents placed into him, the proxies evoked, and the role toward which he is propelled.

If we now consider that absence of positive indicators is nonconfirmatory, positive validation from the patient assumes two basic forms:

1. Positive introjective identifications with the analyst. This is the interactional component of validation. It is based on the patient's sense of being understood and helped, and on the manner in which a correct intervention reflects the constructive inner-directed and outer-directed adaptations of the analyst; it communicates his capacity both to fulfill his responsibilities to the patient and to manage his own inner conflicts, fantasies, introjects, and potential sources of inner disturbance. The patient unconsciously perceives the analyst who has intervened sensitively or has constructively managed the framework as a person with a variety of ego strengths and adaptive capacities. He makes an introjective identification with these aspects, and processes it in accordance with his own intrapsychic needs and fantasies. These experiences in turn help to modify his own inner structures, introjects, and identity—temporarily or more lastingly. On the whole, these identificatory mechanisms contribute to the general ego strength and management capacities of the patient, though in addition they may help develop his capacity to deal with specific intrapsychic conflicts and disturbing unconscious fantasies and memories.

2. The second basic mode of validation is through cognitive confirmatory material from the patient. A correct intervention affords the analysand affectively toned insights into his pathological unconscious processes and contents, insights he then utilizes for adaptive mastery as reflected in more adequate, less symptomatic conflict resolutions and characterological changes. In the

immediate clinical situation, these adaptive inner modifications are reflected in the alteration of repressive barriers
and other pathological defenses. The patient then
communicates fresh material, new associations further
illuminating the area interpreted. Since there is a general
tendency within the analyst to value positively or to
overvalue his interventions, and to read confirmation into
the patient's responses, it is to be stressed that validating
associations must include unexpected and meaningful new
communications from the patient and not simply be
restricted to flat, affirmative pronouncements or rumina-
tions or the repetition of previously known material. In
addition, verbal confirmation should at some point extend
into behavioral change and symptom resolution.

Even where the patient unconsciously needs to refute
essentially valid interventions—for example, because of
unconscious guilt or wishes to defeat the analyst—there
will be embedded in his responses islands of confirmation.
Under these circumstances, the analyst must not only
observe confirmatory identifications and meaningful
verbalized elaborations (most often, they both occur) but
must also perceive material through which the patient's
refutation is itself understood, interpreted, and validated.
On the other hand, immediate negation does not
constitute nonconfirmation, since this conclusion should
be based only on extended observations over time. If an
intervention is not validated, the analyst must reformu-
late, making use both of his own capacities to reassess and
of the patient's associations, which will as a rule provide
him clues regarding his error—and its underlying basis.
The new thesis must then undergo this same validating
process.

It should be recognized that nonvalidation is not the
simple absence of a positive response from the patient;

rather, it involves a complex reaction based on the nature of the erroneous intervention, the inner needs and state of the patient, and the status of the therapeutic interaction. In brief, nonvalidating responses include the following:

1. The absence of cognitive confirmation, usually accompanied by associations—both consciously and unconsciously—intended to guide the analyst toward a correct intervention.

2. Derivative expressions of the patient's negative or pathological introjective identification with the therapist who has erred and with the contents of his error. Incorrect interventions, since they do not pertain primarily to the problems of the patient, reflect the misunderstandings and psychopathology of the analyst. As such, they constitute disturbed communications and projective identifications into the patient by the analyst, derived from the latter's own inner pathological contents; the patient will metabolize these contents in keeping with his own inner state and needs, among many other factors. At such a juncture, the patient's continuing associations in part constitute interactionally the reprojection of the therapist's projective identifications, and often this reflects curative efforts by the patient toward the analyst.

3. Other responses based on inappropriate role evocations prompted by the analyst's intervention; feelings and fantasies related to the analyst's failure to understand the analysand. These may include efforts to exploit the analyst's error to perpetuate the patient's neurosis or other pathology.

Both validating and nonvalidating responses are complex dimensions of the analytic interaction. In applying the validating process, the analyst must monitor his perceptions for distortions based on his own unresolved intrapsychic conflicts, fantasies, and introjects, which disturb both his communications to the patient and his assessment of the analysand's reactions. Constant effort must be made to comprehend both the manifest and the latent content of the patient's communications and behaviors; it is essential to identify the adaptive context for the patient's material in order properly to ascertain its crucial unconscious dimensions. Countertransference-based disturbances are frequent, and may lead the analyst not only to attribute his own inner mental contents, defenses, processes, and introjects to the patient, but also to attempt, unconsciously, to stir up these inner states within the patient through projective identifications and efforts to evoke roles and proxies. There is the danger of inappropriate biases that prompt the analyst to select for his attention, introjection, and interpretation only those contents from the patient that are in keeping with his own pathological complexes, unconscious fantasies, and defensive needs.

Confinement of one's thinking to manifest content is a common blind spot. The unencumbered analyst, on the other hand, generally will approach the ideal of listening, intervening, and validating in a relatively undistorted and insightful manner, essentially in keeping with the therapeutic needs of the patient. Ultimately, the entire process relies on the analyst's awareness of his sensitivities and areas of competence or vulnerability, his potential blind spots, and his reactions to particular types of patients or material. He must strive to know his own personal equation and to maintain an adequate level of management of his inevitable inner difficulties, which, ideally, should not be overintense. Above all, the analyst must be prepared to recognize and accept indications that he is in error, and to explore and modify his views.

The Validating Process within the Patient. There is considerable evidence that because the patient in analysis or therapy experiences a deep need to understand himself and to find release from mental suffering, he therefore consciously and unconsciously endeavors to validate his own formulations about his inner experiences and processes. These can be highly intellectualized and defensive, but they are by no means inherently so and may at times reflect considerable sensitivity. In addition, each patient will attempt on some level to validate his analyst's interventions and management, assessing the influence on his inner state and behaviors. His approach is basically like that of the psychoanalyst, although the level of awareness tends to be more constricted and the cues that he uses are usually quite different. In general, much of this process occurs on an unconscious level and through less explicit and precise clues and formulations.

There are many avenues of validation available to the patient. For instance, he may compare a given communication from the analyst with previous statements and subsequent interventions. Though he does not in general have the capacity to garner as much conscious information as the analyst, the analysand does have many available cues and some capacity for unconscious perception, introjection, and sensitivity that enrich his comprehension of the analyst's intermittent communications, including his silences. He can also observe his own verbalized associations to the analyst's interventions and may even be aware of aspects of his own inner state that he does not communicate openly. Thus, the patient has available to him as a basis for validation observations both of the analyst and of his own inner experience.

Since validation by the patient has been rather neglected, some elaboration is in order. While the analyst's responsibility along these lines requires that he consciously make efforts and develop skills at validation, leaving room only secondarily for unconscious processing, it is characteristic for the patient to utilize primarily unconscious cues; his conscious perceptions and assessments tend to be less reliable. In the course of an analysis, the differences between patient and analyst in this respect should diminish, especially as the analysand develops a heightened awareness of previously unconscious sensitivities. This is accomplished, in part, by modification of the patient's pathological defenses—especially those of repression and denial; by his increasing unconscious identification with the analytic methods undertaken by the analyst; and by his growing awareness and openness to unconscious contents.

Despite the limited data available to the patient, he does have specific means for assessing his reactions to an intervention and its influence on him. He becomes aware of shifts in his own affective state, of new recollections, of a sense of fit or reorganization, and of new derivatives of unconscious fantasies. His sense of empathic communication with and closeness to the analyst may shift in a positive direction; or he may experience the positive effects of the introjective identification of the contents placed into him by the analyst and of the object representation of the analyst who has provided him a positive inner experience. His intuitive processes, any sense of inner relief or symptom modification, and of course enlargements in his cognitive understanding may also serve as guides. Inevitably, these experiences are processed in accordance with his intrapsychic needs and fantasies, and are subject to distortion, but they do provide an extensive repertoire of reliable means of validating the communications from the analyst, and do have a potentially nondistorted core.

In addition to conscious efforts to assess the qualities of the interventions offered him, clinical observation suggests that the patient in analysis or therapy characteristically attempts to validate these interventions (and important noninterventions) unconsciously. Patients have an exquisite sensitivity in this respect, and it is evident that, ultimately, all efforts at validation are interactional as well as intrapsychic. Indeed, one may trace an interactional sequence in which both analyst and analysand respond to their respective communications with conscious and unconscious efforts at validation, communicate the results of these endeavors, and through various interactional and intrapsychic mechanisms introject and process the outcome. They then further work over these efforts and their outcome as an interactionally shared experience—a product of the bipersonal field. Interactionally, the validating process may therefore be viewed as a product of the bipersonal field, with input from the two participants and their shared experiences. From this vantage point, the analyst's efforts at validation, while primarily based on his own resources, are significantly influenced by the patient, while those of the patient are similarly affected by unconscious communications and projective identifications from the analyst. Thus, in addition to unilateral, intrapsychically-based disturbances in the validating process that may occur in either participant, there also may be shared interactional blind spots and disturbances— expressions of the pathology of the field. Finally, interactional validation may be a widening process developed by sequential contributions from the patient and analyst, or it may suffer disturbances based on the resistances and pathological needs of either member of the dyad. As a rule, this will either lead to a shared resistance or will prompt unconscious curative efforts in the other participant, whether patient or analyst, in an effort to strengthen the validating potential of the field, that is, of each participant. The analyst can make good use of the patient's validating endeavors.

With these important interactional considerations in mind, we may conclude our discussion of the validating process with a final point. The analyst is operating within a generally valid and previously verified theoretical framework, and with an understanding of himself and others that has come from his own analysis. I have left this element until last, since the analyst should not operate through rigid, unmodifiable theories, but should subject them to daily efforts at verification. There is the ever-present danger that the analyst will confirm only those ideas he brings to the analytic situation, and that validation will serve as a false front for self-fulfilling prophesises. It should be instead the personal experience of every analyst that his consistent use of the validating process, as shared with each of his patients, will foster his personal and professional development and consistently enlarge his sphere of comprehension of both himself and his patients. The validating process is the key to such growth, not only for the individual analyst but for the broad development of basic psychoanalytic theory and technique.

Having established the applicability of this synthesis to both the psychotherapeutic and psychoanalytic situations, and having provided the validating process as a secure foundation, I now turn directly to the task of describing the components and qualities of the therapeutic relationship and interaction.

Chapter 2

The Bipersonal Field
and Its Frame

The relationship and interaction between the patient and the analyst occurs in the context of a relatively well-defined psychological, temporal, and physical setting—the analytic space or the bipersonal field. The framework of this field creates the essential conditions for the analytic work and must be considered in some detail before we attempt artifically to isolate the two polarities of this bipersonal field—the patient and the analyst. Even the attempt to discuss this framework separately does an injustice to the wholeness of the bipersonal field and the analytic relationship for at least two reasons: first, the patient and especially the analyst form living parts of the frame; second, interactions related to the framework overlap and are on a continuum with the other transactions between the two participants.

It is for these reasons too that the frame in many ways defies the use of metaphor. Viewing it as analogous to the frame of a painting that sets off the reality within from the reality without brings forth images that are both too rigid and too lacking in depth and in human qualities. The three-dimensional analogy to a marine tank or some other type of inanimate container also fails to hold up in some important respects and is too rigid for comparison with the analytic framework. Perhaps the closest we may come for the moment to representing this framework is to think of it as a multifaceted human container and living institution which sets the boundaries of the analytic relationship, creates the rules of the interaction, establishes the nature of the realities and fantasies that occur within it, offers an effective hold and means of security for the participants, defines the therapeutic qualities of the field, contributes to the nature of the communicative network within its confines, and generates certain selected anxieties in the participants as well.

The frame generates unconscious meanings for both patient and analyst, and extensively influences every facet of their interaction. By isolating a space or interactional field into which most outside influences may enter solely through the participants, the frame is relatively closed, and all points are potentially under the influence and reflect the state of all others. This is of great importance in comprehending the analytic interaction. It is the presence and nature of the frame that creates the type of definitive analytic situation within which the patient has the greatest opportunity for inner structural change.

The Components of the Frame-Container

It is the implicit and explicit ground rules and boundaries, including certain basic attitudes of the analyst, that distinguish a given analytic situation from the rest of the world and contribute to the solidarity of the frame, its containing functions, and the conditions prevailing within it. The components of the frame-container may be divided roughly into those that are animate or human— stemming largely though not entirely from the analyst— and those that are more inanimate or nonhuman, though not entirely divorced from the participants, consisting mainly of the fixed arrangements. These components may be classified as follows:

1. The fixed arrangements and relative constants: (a) the physical location of the analyst's office and the confinement of verbal exchanges to his consultation room, while the patient is on the couch; (b) the placement of the patient on the couch and of the analyst out of sight behind him (in psychotherapy, of course, both participants are usually in chairs, face to face); (c) set fee, hours, and length of session, including a determined frequency of sessions each week; (d) the fundamental rule of free association for the analysand, and the free-floating attention and controlled role responsiveness of the analyst; (e) the absence of physical contact; (f) the exclusive one-to-one relationship, with total confidentiality.

2. The human components of the frame. While it is evident that some of the above ground rules include significant personal elements, the following aspects of the frame-container rely largely on the functions of the analyst, who may be assisted or hindered in those efforts by the analysand: (a) his offer of a basic hold for the patient and a container for his pathology, based on his concern as a physician or healer, his steady qualities, and his capacity to understand and intervene; (b) his relative anonymity; (c) his position equidistant from all psychic structures and reality; (d) his use of neutral interventions geared primarily toward interpretation; (e) his capacity to offer the patient appropriate gratifications—primarily through his management of the frame and the offer of valid

interpretations—and to preclude extratherapeutic, inappropriate gratifications.

These ground rules, boundaries, and attitudes define the nature of the analytic bipersonal field. They are by no means rigid commandments or absolute laws, but are sound, clinically validated tenets that create the best conditions for the patient's analytic experience—a secure hold, a viable container, and a field with optimal therapeutic qualities and openness of communication.

The Establishment of
the Framework-Container

There are a number of means through which the frame is created. First, there is the analyst's initial attitude, concern, and ability to intervene early where necessary. There is also his creation of a formal agreement—the analytic pact—with the analysand as it is explicated by the analyst's implicit and explicit communications.

As the analytic experience unfolds—especially during the initial phase, but throughout the analysis—there will be repeated tests of the frame, and its holding and containing functions. While most of these derive from the patient, they are not uncharacteristic for the analyst as well, and depend on experiences within and outside the analytic situation which stir up a variety of needs and anxieties related to the framework.

It is characteristic for all patients to test the analyst's management of the ground rules and boundaries, and to endeavor to modify them as a means of obtaining noninsightful symptom relief and inappropriate gratification(*framework cures*—a form of *misalliance cure*; see below). The analysis of such efforts relies first on the analyst's capacity to maintain the frame, and second, on his ability to interpret the unconscious meanings of the patient's endeavors to modify it. From time to time, the analyst himself will struggle—internally and, one hopes, on only rare occasions in actuality—with wishes to modify the frame. In general, he should control such tendencies and instead should engage in a period of self-analysis as a means of understanding the relevant unconscious motives.

In this context, we may note that when faced with the analyst's inappropriate needs to modify the framework, it is characteristic for the patient to respond in mixed fashion. In general, he will initially accept the framework cure that has been offered and momentarily perpetuate the sector of misalliance involved; later, he will introject the pathological projective identifications effected by the analyst's modification in the frame, and become involved in curative efforts directed at the analyst-introject and at the analyst, endeavoring to assist him with the countertransference difficulties that have prompted the inappropriate alteration of the framework.

The patient's need for a secure frame, hold, and container is great, and it may be relied upon in those situations where either patient or analyst suggest an alteration. Under such circumstances, as long as the analyst does not commit himself in advance to the modification and maintains the bipersonal field open for conscious and unconscious communications pertaining to the proposed request, the patient's unconscious communications will convey the pathological elements involved. Technically, this means that the analyst may be assured of obtaining derivatives from the patient that provide analyzable material regarding the neurotic gratifications involved in an alteration in the frame, and he can interpret and often trace the genetic basis of such material, and utilize it as a clear indication from the patient for the actual need to maintain the framework. Such analytic experiences, in which interpretations of the unconscious meanings of the frame and its proposed alteration prevail, and in which the analyst in reality maintains the security of the frame, are critical to the secure establishment of a therapeutic bipersonal field.

The holding and containing functions of the frame are created through a variety of transactions with the analysand. The holding qualities are conveyed implicitly and explicitly through the analyst's tolerance, patience, and his ability to respond in nondisruptive and nonretaliatory ways to the patient's initial threats, attacks, or efforts at seduction. The ability to maintain unswerving attitudes of concern, benevolence, anonymity, and neutrality, and to respond interpretively, is crucial. Similarly, the analyst's capacity to contain the patient's pathology and especially his pathological projective identifications is established through his openness to such communications, his ability to offer an analytic situation in which the patient is free to express sickness both verbally and interactionally, and through his ways of indicating the positive qualities of his containing efforts. These are imparted to the patient through proper interpretations of unconscious fantasies and pathological interactional efforts vis-à-vis the analyst. Such interventions reflect the analyst's ability to metabolize the patient's projective identifications properly: cognitively, they indicate his understanding of these disturbing contents, while interactionally they reflect his ability to introjectively identify with the patient's pathological projective identifications and to reproject healthier, constructively modified contents for the patient's introjection. When the analyst is refractory as a container for the patient's pathology or is unable to properly metabolize the patient's projective identifications, he will disrupt the patient's communications in a variety of ways and be unable to interpret the nature and meanings of the patient's pathological communications and projective identifications (see below).

In all, the establishment of the frame relies on certain basic, constructive attitudes in the analyst, his ability to manage and interpret the inevitable tests in this sphere, and on the implicit demonstration of his containing and interpretive abilities.

The Implications and Ramifications of the Framework

As I have noted, the frame as boundary, hold, and container influences virtually every aspect of the analytic relationship and interaction. Its management is therefore crucial to the outcome of the more formal, verbally-based analytic efforts, and for the analytic resolution of the pathological efforts at interaction initiated by the patient toward the analyst in spheres other than that related to the frame itself. Because of its pervasive influence, patients are remarkably sensitive to the most minimal alteration in the frame; and because of its fundamental role in the analytic situation, the actual *rectification* of an altered frame and the analysis of the implications of such a modification take general precedence over all other analytic work. Here, I will briefly list the main functions, influences, and ramifications of the framework:

1. The frame is basic to the analytic matrix, and is an aspect of matrix transference and nontransference, and matrix countertransference and noncountertransference (see chapters 3 and 4). In this regard, it is to be noted again

that the analytic frame has crucial human elements derived from the patient and especially the analyst.

2. The frame is the living institution that defines the analytic field, the nature and flow of communications within it, the areas of gratification and renunciation for its participants, and the controls necessary for both in order to create the best possible analytic interaction. It is therefore under constant pressure from the neurotic needs and pathogenic unconscious wishes of both patient and analyst.

3. It is a basic component of the fundamental hold through which the analyst provides the patient with the security, trust, stability, tolerance, support, and safeguards he needs both to garner the basic ego strength required for analytic work and to reveal his conscious and unconscious pathological impulses, introjects, and fantasies.

4. The frame defines the optimal distance for both participants in the relationship and creates the conditions for the development of an interface of communication between them.

5. It is the behavioral and institutional guide that gears the relationship toward verbalization, analyzable interactions, cognitive insight, and constructive introjective identifications for the patient, and to a lesser extent, for the analyst. In essence, it creates the therapeutic qualities of the field and renders it safe for the communication of pathological needs and derivatives, and serves as the guarantor of their analyzability and use toward therapeutic ends. It therefore affects what is communicated by both participants, its implications and meanings, and the responses of both members of the analytic dyad. Within a valid frame, all communications and behaviors of the patient are treated as material for analysis and interpreta-

tion; direct, inappropriate response or gratification is precluded. In this way, the frame insures what has been termed the *transference illusion*, the nongratification of the patient's inappropriate and "neurotic"—pathological— wishes, and renders the patient free to safely communicate all aspects of his conscious and unconscious inner life.

6. The management of the framework by the analyst reflects his ability to respond to the needs of the patient and the qualities of his own inner state, unconscious fantasies, needs and conflicts, and the extent to which they have been adequately controlled and managed from within. As such, it is one nonverbal mode through which the analyst communicates the status of his intrapsychic balances and thus influences both the patient's identificatory processes and his pursuit of insight. The patient's responses to the frame reflect comparable factors regarding his own inner state and impart similar communications to the analyst.

7. As a real institution, embedded in behavior and actuality, the framework is fundamental to the analytic interaction. Its impact takes precedence over verbalized communication and especially the manifest content of such communications. The fantasies, ego and superego functions, self-image, and object relatedness of the analyst, as communicated in his management of the framework, convey meanings that the patient consistently monitors, largely unconsciously, and these meanings are a first order of communication between the two participants. Only when this level forms a consistent and constructive backdrop do the analyst's verbal interventions have their intended implications and effects.

8. The frame defines the "screen" onto which the patient projects his intrapsychic fantasies, influencing the nature, openness, and availability of the analyst in his

function as a screen. It also establishes the conditions for the projections and projective identifications, and the introjections and introjective identifications, of both participants. On one hand, the management of the frame generates specific projective identifications—positively or negatively toned—from the analyst into the patient; on the other, it affects the implications of all such interactional processes.

9. The frame not only influences the analyzability of the expressions from the patient and the interpretive qualities of the analyst's interventions, it also offers safeguards for patient and analyst. By providing boundaries and limits, and defining the field as essentially therapeutic, the framework offers ego strength and support to both patient and analyst to sustain the analytic work and, more broadly, to effect positive introjective identifications. It is these positive elements, derived from the consistency of the frame, its holding and containing capacities expressed through the medium of the analyst, that enable him to utilize the frame therapeutically. Thus, the maintenance of a secure frame and the rectification of a modified one constitute therapeutic interventions with powerful non-verbal implications capable of strengthening the patient's ego and of modifying aspects of his unconscious fantasies.

10. By establishing the scope of what will transpire between the patient and analyst, the framework determines how the patient's relationship with the analyst and his self-expressions will unfold. It is therefore a relatively reliable and steady guide to the temporal transactions of the analysis. In addition to the unconscious meanings and functions of the total framework, each specific ground rule and boundary is experienced and perceived by both patient and analyst in terms of diverse unconscious implications and fantasies. Each serves to direct and limit an aspect of

the analytic interaction, and may be utilized constructively or misused for neurotic gain.

11. The fundamental rule of free association, for instance, as a central component of the analytic pact, promotes the abolition of repression and other defenses in the patient, encourages the more open expression of his intrapsychic conflicts and instinctual-drive derivatives, places the analyst in a special and privileged position, and exposes him to primitive derivatives and impulses—to identify but a few of its unconscious implications. The payment of fees, the time limit to the sessions, the analyst's neutrality and relative anonymity, and the totally confidential one-to-one relationship are filled with meaning for both participants, and may be silently accepted or enter into the patient's—or analyst's— intrapsychic conflicts and become part of the pathogenic interaction between the two. As a rule, it is when there is a disturbance in an aspect of a particular ground rule or boundary that its unconscious meanings and functions come to the fore, requiring both rectification where necessary, and full analysis.

12. The framework creates the container for the patient's pathological contents and interaction. The maintenance of each ground rule and boundary is essential to the development of the analyst's containing functions, capacities that have to do with his receptivity to the patient's pathological projective identifications, pathological interactions, and pathological contents. The openness of the analyst's containing functions relies on his management of the framework and the introjective identification of the pathological contents from the patient, with subsequent metabolism and interpretation. As a rule, modifications in the frame express a refractoriness or disruptive openness by the analyst to contain

aspects of the patient's pathological contents and projective identifications, and are often motivated by such unconscious needs.

13. Finally, with all of the stress in the literature on the positive and maternal qualities of a secure framework and analytic hold, it is important to make note of the anxieties and conflicts evoked by the establishment of a well-defined and proper framework. The creation of such a bipersonal field implies potentially anxiety-provoking intimacy with the analyst and pressures the patient toward regression and the experience of his own disturbing pathological unconscious contents. In addition, a secure frame implies the absence of gratification of the patient's neurotic needs, and while this is welcomed on one level, considerable protest is expressed on another—largely through efforts to modify the frame. In all, then, a secure frame creates a situation in which the patient's usual maladaptive resources are challenged or thwarted, and it generates anxiety regarding the failure of his usual defenses and the exposure of his dreaded inner world, as well as a feared dependency on the analyst. Similarly, for the analyst, a secure frame implies the nongratification of his neurotic needs, the modification of his own maladaptive coping mechanisms and defenses, a limited regression that exposes him to his own and to the analysand's primitive contents, and the potential for anxiety related to disturbing aspects of his limited intimacy with the patient and the patient's dependency on him.

Overall, both patient and analyst enter the analytic relationship divided: one part wishing for cure, the other for the status quo, the maintenance of the neurosis or other form of illness. Hopefully, the proportions of these needs differ within each, so that the analyst's curative wishes and capacities far outweigh those related to his wishes for the patient to be sick. However, through such neurotic needs and other disturbed motives, again in varying degrees, both patient and analyst, while they welcome the positive attributes of a secure framework, also desire to disrupt that security. There are, therefore, continuous pressures in both participants to inappropriately modify the frame in order to interrupt the psychoanalytic work, and to provide inappropriate gratification and defenses. There similarly are strong urges to modify such maladaptive thrusts and to restore the ascendancy of insightful cure. In a sense, the fate of the frame determines the fate of the analysis.

Management of the Framework: Technical Aspects

Recognition of the pervasive influence of the framework on the therapeutic interaction and process endow with great significance the analyst's management and interpretations of the unconscious factors in any effort by either participant to modify the frame. It is clear that the basic need for a secure framework which creates the proper holding and containing conditions of the therapeutic situation, and provides the bipersonal field with its essential therapeutic characteristics, prevails in both the psychoanalytic and psychotherapeutic situations. Here, I will briefly outline the clinical issues that arise in connection with the management of the framework, and indicate the consequences of various alternatives for both the patient and the analyst:

1. The analyst should constantly monitor the state of the framework and each of its components: its holding functions, its containing functions, its role in creating a distinctive boundary for the analytic situation, and its

contributions to the therapeutic qualities of the field. Technically, this implies quiet attention to the various ground rules and boundaries, including an assessment of his own interventions in order to determine whether they have in any way modified his anonymity, neutrality, or attitude of not gratifying the patient's or his own inappropriate wishes.

2. The analyst is assisted in his management of the frame by the analysand, who also—largely unconsciously—monitors this aspect of the analytic relationship and tests it from time to time. In evaluating the patient's associations for relevant unconscious communications, the analyst should consistently examine them for direct and especially indirect allusions to the framework and its status. Disturbances in the frame originating from any source will impinge upon the patient and prompt pervasive, though often indirect, responses.

3. While leaving room for flexibility, the needs of the analysand call for a consistent maintenance of a relatively unaltered frame to provide the essential setting for analytic work and adaptive inner change.

(a) The analyst should endeavor to maintain the basic aspects of the frame—his neutrality, anonymity, total confidentiality, the one-to-one relationship, and the like— as essentially unchanging, and should be prepared to rectify and analyze minor infringements as they inevitably occur in the course of an analysis.

(b) Minor requests to restructure the frame—for example, a necessary shift to a new hour—should be handled by initial nonagreement, direct and indirect exploration of the patient's subsequent associations and behaviors with the request in mind as the adaptive context, and both a full analytic exploration of the implications for the analysand and the use of the material as a guide for the actual decision. While some flexibility is necessary, the patient's unconscious communications and the realities of the situation should guide the analyst in his decision. Even in those situations where the realities are unmistakable, some alteration in the therapeutic functions of the field and in the viable properties of the analytic situation may follow such a change, and may need either further rectification or additional analytic exploration and understanding. In general, whatever realities prompt an alteration in the frame, some degree of disturbance and inappropriate gratification will accrue to both participants, a small portion of which may remain unresolved.

(c) All other efforts by the analysand to modify the frame and all impulses in this direction within the analyst should, wherever possible, not be actualized, and instead should be frustrated by the analyst and subjected to full analytic exploration. Participation in a modification of the frame by the analyst, especially when this is knowingly undertaken, will modify the therapeutic qualities of the field and the openness of the patient's communications, and thereby preclude analytic investigation toward insight regarding the unconscious implications of the alteration. Such participation also reinforces the maladaptive defenses and inappropriate gratifications entailed in modifying the frame.

(d) The analyst should be prepared to maintain the basic frame except for extreme emergencies, and then only with great caution and after all other measures have failed. Emergency measures should be undertaken judiciously and subjected to subsequent rectification and full analytic exploration at the earliest possible moment. Consequences for the patient, the therapeutic field, and the analytic work will, nonetheless, be considerable, and some portion of it may be unmodifiable.

4. When the patient unilaterally modifies the frame—through lateness, absence, nonpayment of fees, physical contact, and the like—it becomes a prime therapeutic context for intervening and a central adaptive context for organizing the patient's subsequent material. The analyst's basic stance is that of nonparticipation; his efforts are toward analytic understanding and rectification, and working through.

(a) Such efforts are among the most powerful attempts of the analysand at noninsightful, maladpative "self-cure"—*framework cures.* The frame not only offers an opportunity for fruitful analytic work, but also creates anxieties related to regression, the awareness of inner dreaded content, and the unconscious meanings of the relationship with the analyst. Therefore, patients will from time to time attempt to alleviate these pressures by modifying the frame. It is a striking clinical finding that such an alteration provides considerable immediate symptom relief, inappropriate gratification, and reinforcement of pathological defenses; analytic work in which these aspects are understood and identified from the patient's associations is especially effective in restricting the utilization of such so-called acting out—living out—and acting in.

(b) These modifications in the framework entail the living out of unconscious fantasies. However, in addition to their fantasy implications, they constitute the invocation of an actuality that modifies the basic therapeutic qualities of the bipersonal field, substantially reinforces pathological defenses, and inappropriately gratifies the patient, thereby momentarily precluding the usual analytic work toward insight—that is, modification of the frame is a reality-based alternative to insight-pursuant analytic work.

(c) In addition to serving as a conscious and unconscious communication that requires rectification and interpretation by the analyst, the patient's modification of the frame creates interactional pressures for him that center largely upon the use of these behaviors as a means of projectively identifying into the analyst a variety of inner fantasies in an effort to evoke a proxy response from him, and as pressure to toward having him assume certain inappropriate roles in response to the analysand—for example, to respond as a forbidding, superego figure or as a corrupted participant. In intervening, the analyst should take cognizance of these interactional mechanisms and efforts, experience them in attenuated—not lived out—form, and interpret them to the patient, rather than consciously or unconsciously participating in a pathological sequence of projective identification, introjective identification, and reprojection—termed *projective counteridentification.*

(d) Any knowing or unknowing participation by the analyst in an inappropriate modification of the frame constitutes a sector of misalliance that will alter the therapeutic qualities of the field, create shared defenses that constitute interactional resistances, constitute bastions of the bipersonal field that entail split-off sectors that are mutually avoided, interfere with the communicative flow of the field, and inappropriately gratify both participants. The presence of a sector of misalliance based on an inappropriate modification of the fame can be detected through the monitoring of the framework, the patient's unconscious communications which as a rule will pertain both to the acceptance of the altered frame and the wish to rectify it, and from subjective clues within the analyst. Such a situation calls for rectification—the cessation of the analyst's participating in the misalliance—

and a full interpretation of its meanings, intrapsychically and interactionally, for the analysand. At such times, *implicit* acceptance of the analyst's participation is called for, without direct acknowledgment or confession. The patient's material will provide ample opportunity for the analyst's interpretive endeavors and should be maintained as the guide for the analytic work.

5. When the analyst inadvertently or knowingly modifies the frame, he may expect in most cases that the patient will accept the misalliance so contained and then unconsciously endeavor to assist him in correcting the situation through a variety of curative efforts. As a rule, such modifications communicate the following to the patient: the analyst's incapacity to manage his own inner state, conflicts, and pathogenic unconscious fantasies and introjects; a projective identification into the patient of the analyst's pathology—his disruptive unconscious fantasies and introjects; a shift in the interface of the bipersonal field toward the pathology of the analyst and in the therapeutic efforts of the field toward his cure; an alteration in the analyst's basic hold of the patient with the resultant general weakening of the latter's ego functioning; and a reluctance or refusal to contain the pathological contents of the analysand.

Important clues regarding the transference-based unconscious motivations that prompt the analyst to inappropriately modify the frame can be found not only through his self-analysis, but also in the material from the patient, which often serves as a precipitant or an adaptive context for the erroneous intervention. The entire constellation produces a negative introjective identification with the sick parts of the analyst, which the patient will characteristically both exploit for his own neurotic needs and attempt to cure. It is incumbent upon the analyst to identify his modification of the frame, to recognize the therapeutic misalliance that it creates with the analysand, to identify the unconscious communication, fantasies, and interactional pressures it contains, and to both rectify the altered frame and interpret all of the implications of the experience for the analysand. It is especially helpful for the analyst to recognize the patient's therapeutic endeavors and, while not directly acknowledging them, demonstrate implicitly the gains that he has made by utilizing them in his own efforts at rectification and interpretation.

6. When the analyst maintains a secure and relatively unmodified frame, the patient experiences the analyst as securely holding and offering an open and constructive container for his pathological contents, affording a series of introjective identifications that provide basic ego strengths and positive introjects related to various ego, superego, and ego ideal systems. The patient is then able to develop a capacity of his own to hold and contain both himself and others, to strengthen the management of his inner fantasies and instinctual drives, to create and maintain appropriate boundaries in his object relationships, and to renounce inappropriate instinctual-drive expressions. While these inherent gains are broad and generally nonspecific, they are reinforced by the details of the analyst's interpretations as related to the frame; this provides the patient with specific cognitive insights into the diverse meanings and functions of the framework as they relate to his intrapsychic conflicts and pathological unconscious fantasies and introjects. Lastly, in actuality, the maintenance of the framework by the analyst offers the patient an interaction that runs contrary to experiences within past pathogenic relationships, implicitly offering new perspectives and new opportunities for positive

identification and inner change. By contrast, unneeded modifications of the frame generate sectors of misalliance that repeat past pathogenic interactions—for both participants—and create for the patient an inappropriate external reality that confirms pathological aspects of his present internal reality and unconscious fantasies.

Concluding Remarks

The framework of the analytic situation may be considered its basic medium. It is derived from virtually every aspect of the analytic situation and relationship and, in turn, influences all of its components. It is by no means inert or rigid, but is a dynamic, fluctuating boundary and set of conditions that the analyst makes every effort to maintain at an effective level and to restore when deviations occur. It is created through the humanity and limited flexibility of the analyst, whose appropriate firmness is in no sense rigidity, but is instead the ultimate expression of his responsibility to create the special conditions under which valid analytic work can take place. Management of the frame requires exceptional renunciation on the part of the analyst and creates necessary burdens for the analysand, yet its maintenance is the cornerstone of the therapeutic process. It is a multifaceted actuality whose alterations require both rectification—the correction of the disturbing reality—and interpretation; it is a special form of unconscious communication, and efforts to change its qualities convey both intrapsychic and interactional meanings.

In the presence of a modified frame, there is a split-off, shared defensive bastions and sectors of misalliance; characteristically, the communicative properties of the field are altered and there is a hollow quality to the analytic work; analyzable derivatives are rare and quickly covered over or defended. The patient continues to free-associate as a rule, but there is a sense of stalemate and superficiality; the available meaningful derivatives relate to the patient's unconscious perceptions of and fantasies about the modified frame. There is a compromised quality to the image of the analyst, to the therapeutic nature of the bipersonal field, and to the outcome of the analytic work. Beyond these potentially temporary changes, certain permanent modifications in the framework or major alterations will have a lasting and limiting effect on analytic outcome. Considerable research is still needed to determine those modifications of the frame that temporarily or permanently compromise analytic work and results.

Finally, it is well to remember that the analytic bipersonal field is designed for the analytic resolution of the patient's symptoms and characterological disturbances. No matter how extensive the analyst's contribution to an altered frame and to a sector of misalliance, in his work with the patient he should not dwell on his countertransference problems and their influence on the analysis—his cure is not the primary therapeutic task or responsibility. Instead he should recognize the presence of a problem and its expression in the alteration of the frame, attempt to understand the implications of his error both in terms of its unconscious sources within himself and its meaningful reflections of aspects of the analysand's inner state—that is, the kernels of constructive responsiveness contained within an essentially disruptive intervention. He should rectify the situation, implicitly accept his responsibility, to the extent that it is realistic to do so, and ultimately return to the analysis of the patient. Much of this depends on the analyst's coming to terms with the anxiety-provoking qualities of a secure frame for himself, and his ability to self-analytically resolve these anxieties, thereby renouncing his inappropriate needs in his relationship with the patient. In this way, he becomes comfortable with the frame—its positive potential and inevitable threat—and the bulk of the analytic work comes to be centered, as it should be, on the analysand.

Chapter 3

The Patient's Relationship
to the Analyst

Having established the properties of the analytic bipersonal field, we may now turn to one of the two participants—the patient. Essentially, his relationship and reactions to the analyst, expressed directly or indirectly, may be identified in terms of transference and nontransference components. The two are, however, on a continuum: there are no clear demarcations, but shadings and intermixtures, so that any comparison between them must deal with relatively idealized concepts. In most clinical situations it is nonetheless possible to distinguish aspects of the patient's relationship to his analyst that are primarily transference-based from those that are not. For heuristic purposes, I shall consider the two separately. Furthermore, although I am essentially describing the patient's *reactions*, it must be borne in mind that his inner set will prompt him to evoke stimuli and behaviors from the analyst that are in keeping with his needs, and also will determine his interpretation of the prevailing realities. On the other hand, external reality, through the analyst and secondarily through others, will impose upon the patient a variety of adaptive tasks to which he will respond. With this in mind, let us begin our dissection of the analytic relationship from the vantage point of the analysand.

The Transference Component

Transference may be defined as that aspect of the patient's adaptive efforts within the analytic situation that is primarily based on the distorting effects of his unconscious fantasies, memories, and introjects, expressed in inappropriate needs, defenses, reactions, perceptions, and the like. Transferences express the ultimate influence of disturbing genetic experiences and relationships on the patient's interaction with the analyst, and drive him toward inappropriate responses to adaptive stimuli that exist within the analytic relationship or are funnelled into it from outside. Such effects may appear directly in the analytic interaction in a relatively manifest form—verbally or behaviorally-interactionally—or may appear through disguised and defended derivatives that pertain directly to the analytic relationship or are expressed through displacements onto other persons and situations. In essence, then, transference consists of those unconscious fantasies about, wishes toward, and reactions to the analyst that reflect some intrapsychic alteration or distortion of the prevailing realities.

There is a transference component in every single communication—verbal associations and behaviors—from the patient to the analyst. Transference-based reactions are by no means restricted to direct responses or references to the analyst or to obvious displacements of such allusions, but appear in many forms and on many levels in the course of any given session. Within an adaptational-interactional framework, it may be recognized that the intensity of the patient's transference responses derives from the exquisitely sensitive and important relationship that he develops with his analyst, and from the related mobilization of a hierarchy of introjects, instinctual drive needs, and concomitant defenses and superego expressions—crystallized into a series of unconscious fantasies and their manifestations. These adaptively aroused transference expressions contribute positively to the analytic work: they are an important motive force in the development of the therapeutic alliance—though not the exclusive motivational factor, since others derive from appropriate, nontransference-based wishes for understanding, cure, and symptom relief (see below). They also provide a means through which the analysand communicates the nature of his psychopathology in a form that is available for analytic work and resolution. In addition, transference-based responses create formidable resistances to analytic progress, in the form of inappropriate instinctual-drive wishes, pathological defenses, and other disruptive qualities that are to be found in the communicative and interactional consequences of these responses.

Transference reactions are based on a very special and intense cathexis by the patient of his relationship with the analyst as a healing figure who stirs up, selectively and nonpathologically gratifies but largely frustrates, needs related to every psychosexual level of development and every aspect of object relatedness. While some minimal degree of satisfaction of unconscious transference fantasies and wishes is inevitable in every analytic experience, this does not constitute a major sector of appropriate gratification for the analysand, i.e., gratification primarily related to reasonable, nontransference needs and wishes. It is primarily the special qualities of the analytic framework and of the analyst's interpretations that create the conditions of deprivation-in-intimacy under which a therapeutic and analyzable transference regression takes place. The interpretive modification of the patient's usual defenses, as well as of pathological superego and ego ideal expressions, also contributes to this therapeutic movement, which can occur, however, only in the context of a secure analytic hold fostering the patient's sense of safety and trust vis-à-vis essential nontransference-related nutriment.

In general, the communication of analyzable derivatives of unconscious transference fantasies depends on the analyst's maintenance of the framework, his ability to identify and interpret resistances, his capacity to incorporate and contain the patient's pathology, and his offer of valid interventions. Under such conditions, the patient's material will continually reflect transference responses as part of his effort to adapt to his relationship with the analyst—and to the latter's verbal and nonverbal communications—and to adjust to his own continuing inner tensions, anxieties, and fantasies.

There are a wide number of classifications of transference, and here I shall explore those that seem most important clinically.

Matrix and Reactive Transferences

Perhaps the most fundamental classification of transference is the distinction between *matrix* and *reactive* transference components. While, as we have come to expect, these two types of transference are on a continuum, the extremes are identifiable and important to recognize.

Matrix Transference. It seems advisable to discuss separately the patient's fundamental relationship with the analyst, the backdrop for his continuing analytic experience. The totality of this basic relationship, as it is shared by the two participants in the analytic situation, is best termed the *matrix relationship.* In terms of the patient's contributions, it has transference and nontransference, distorted and reality-based components—each with important genetic counterparts. The matrix relationship contributes significantly to the therapeutic alliance and, when impaired, is a major factor in disruptions of that alliance and of the analytic work.

The transference components of the matrix relationship draw upon each of the types of transference to be described below, and while the most fundamental level is that of the primordial and symbiotic transference elements, there are contributions from every stage of psychosexual development and every phase of self- and object-relations. Matrix transference is characterized by a slow rate of change in comparison to reactive transference; it is responsive to and modifiable by analytic work only after extensive periods of working through. It contributes to preformed transferences—the transference component of the patient's expectations when seeking analysis—and is subsequently reinforced or modified by the actualities of the analytic experience, including the personality of the analyst, his handling of the relationship, his interventions, his management of the framework, and the like.

Matrix transference expressions are, by definition, inappropriate and distorting; in a given analytic situation, they may be quite significant or minor. This form of transference relates to basic wishes for instinctual-drive gratification, fusion, and closeness. Although inappropriate and tied to pathogenic genetic elements, when they are not overintense, such wishes may contribute to the so-called "sublimated positive transference" and thereby further the analytic work and therapeutic alliance for a period of time. These positively toned aspects include derivatives of earlier interactions that directly and defensively contribute to distortions in the patient's expectations and view of the analyst, such as the search for magical healing, idealizations, or blind trust. These transference elements may be intensified or perpetuated by inadvertent or inevitable gratifications from the analyst, and by erroneous interventions and mismanagements of the frame. As transference expressions related to the patient's psychopathology, however, ultimately they must not be gratified but be modified analytically, lest they contribute to major unresolved resistances.

It is to be noted that matrix transference is only one—relatively treacherous—aspect of the patient's trust of the analyst. Feelings of trust are based on earlier adequate experiences with the patient's mothering figure and other supportive individuals, and subsequent intrapsychic elaborations within the patient—that is, they have important nontransference elements. The distorted aspects lead to inappropriately positive images of the analyst and extend beyond the actualities of his functioning, and include projections onto him of good, though distorted, introjects. If the analyst conducts himself in a sound, appropriate, and effective manner, he will reinforce the valid, nondistorted, nontransference contributions to this sense of trust. All of these factors contribute to the early therapeutic alliance, and only the inappropriate elements must be subjected eventually to analytic resolution—essentially when they emerge in an analyzable form within an appropriate adaptive and therapeutic context.

There appears to be some tendency to neglect positively

toned, though ultimately pathological, matrix transference expressions. On the other hand, destructive matrix transference elements—we might term them "negative matrix transferences"—tend to undermine the basic therapeutic alliance and essential aspects of the analytic work, and more often command analytic attention. These transferences are based on earlier traumatic experiences and their inner, fantasied elaboration by the patient. This leads to distorted, relatively enduring hostile wishes toward, negative images of, aggressive reactions to, and destructive projections onto the analyst by the patient. Often, this type of matrix transference is expressed in a chronic sense of mistrust of and hostility toward the analyst that is difficult to analyze and resolve.

These relatively basic and enduring matrix transference components are only slowly and gradually influenced by the analyst's stance, interventions, management of the framework, and inevitable errors and insensitivities, as well as by certain painful aspects of his constructive functioning—for example, the hurt sometimes involved in a necessary interpretation and the anxieties evoked by the maintenance of a secure frame. Repeated errors and mismanagement of the frame may confirm and reinforce unconscious matrix transference fantasies, rendering them even more difficult than usual to analyze and resolve, and sometimes turning them into unmodifiable resistances.

The analytic modification of matrix transference components relies first on the analyst's steady and consistent management of the frame and his interpretive work, which provide the patient with insights and introjects that alter this aspect of his transference constellation. In addition, specific incidents within and external to the analysis will generate adaptive contexts and intrapsychic reactions that are pertinent to the genetic experiences and unconscious fantasies on which the matrix transference is founded. Careful analytic work during such periods provides a vehicle for the specific analytic alteration of these basically distorted, relatively durable transference expressions, a process that contributes significantly to modifications in the patient's adaptive resources, self-image, pathological unconscious transference fantasies, and psychopathology.

Reactive Transference. This is composed of the generally fluctuating transference components of all kinds that arise as part of the patient's immediate efforts to adapt to the analyst, the analytic situation, and the outside world—to the extent that they are expressed, directly or indirectly, in distorted unconscious fantasies regarding the analyst. Each patient's transference constellation and its crystallization into a so-called "transference neurosis or syndrome" (a syndrome that, in terms of current loose usage, actually includes admixtures of matrix and reactive transference, and of nontransference components as well) is individually distinctive.

The analysand's transference syndrome may be defined as a reorganization of his emotional symptoms and characterological disturbances around derivatives of distorted unconscious needs, fantasies, defenses, and perceptions related to the analyst. In clinical practice, this syndrome is never free from nontransference influences and of shaping pressures derived from the behaviors of the analyst; it is defined here as a hypothetical ideal. The intensity and other qualities of the transference constellation and its availability for analytic work vary with a wide range of factors. These include those derived from the analysand's past, such as the history of his object relationships, specific acute and repetitive genetic experiences, and past vulnerabilities and strengths; those that are admixtures of the past and present—psychopathology, character structure, intrapsychic conflicts, fantasies, and introjects, and the nature of self and of psychic structures; and those that prevail in present reality—the nature of the frame and of intercurrent reality events, and characteristics of the analyst, such as his personality, character structure, psychopathology, style of working, and technical abilities. Reactive transference components tend to fluctuate in keeping with the patient's current adaptive tasks, the unconscious fantasies and introjects that have been mobilized at a particular time, and the state of his adaptive and maladaptive tendencies.

In the analysis of transference, it is the reactive elements reflected in the patient's associations and behaviors—interactions—that express inevitable resistances and core unconscious fantasies that form the basic field for analytic exploration, interpretation, and working through. These transference components serve all the psychic agencies of the patient: the ego's adaptive functions and defensive needs, the superego and ego ideal systems, and the id, as well as his self-system. The analysand's search for transference gratifications and maladaptive resolution of his unconscious transference fantasies and conflicts creates potential resistances and opportunities for analytic work related to the patient's patient's pathological needs; in addition, these transference expressions may evoke more positive efforts at renunciation and control, and the search for more direct cognitive insights.

It is useful to speak of active and passive reactive transferences, as long as this is not thought to express a sharp distinction. *Active reactive transference* refers to the patient's active, although usually unconscious, efforts to seek out reactions from the analyst and others that would gratify or justify his intrapsychic, unconscious transference fantasies. In addition, they include the patient's need to misinterpret external reality in terms of these intrapsychic fantasies, introjects, and wishes. This active type of reactive transference stems primarily from the patient's intrapsychic defensive and gratifying motives and is akin to Freud's (1923) concept of dreams derived from below.

At the other end of this continuum are those distorted responses in the patient that may be termed *passive reactive transference* expressions. Like dreams from above (Freud 1923), these are transference-based responses that are primarily evoked by external realities, and especially by the behaviors and communications from the analyst. They are then secondarily elaborated upon intrapsychically. It is especially important to distinguish these reactions from nontransference responses that are similarly elaborated intrapsychically but with significantly different implications. Passive reactive transferences are responses to communications from the analyst—not unduly traumatizing or hurtful—and to his maintenance of the frame as they stir up the patient's intrapsychic distorting fantasies. By contrast, in the reality-based or primarily nontransference reaction, the stimulus from the analyst is inherently unnecessarily traumatic, as well as subsequently elaborated in accordance with the patient's transference-based needs. This distinction, which I shall later clarify, has important technical implications despite inevitable overlaps: the nature of the bipersonal field and the locus of its interface, the conscious and unconscious image of the analyst, his therapeutic position, and the balance of the patient's unconscious fantasies and perceptions all differ in important ways in the two circumstances.

Finally, reactive transference responses contain within them both the seeds of the patient's cure and of those factors which may interfere in a major way with or preclude such cure. They contain the elements for constructive inner change on the one hand, and on the other, may be designed to maintain the neurosis. These reactions are central—though not the exclusive therapeutic medium—in both analytic and psychotherapeutic work, and like matrix transferences, may work either toward healthy adaptation or neurotic maladaptation. In determining the ultimate outcome, balances within the analysand that are influenced by the analyst's interpretations and maintenance of the framework play a crucial role, as does the analyst's capacity to identify clearly these elements and to distinguish them from nontransference responses, to manage their interactional expressions, and to interpret their derivative forms within active adaptive contexts.

The Sources of
Transference Reactions

Genetic or Classical Transference.   In keeping with Freud's original definition, *genetic transference* refers to those unconscious distortions of the patient's relationships to the analyst that are derived and displaced from early disruptive childhood relationships and experiences with significant figures, primarily parents, and secondarily siblings and others. The intrapsychic residuals from such acute and cumulative traumas create unconscious sets and a variety of needs and defenses that influence the patient's experiencing, reacting, and perceiving, and in general distort his relationships and interactions. They are especially intensified by the conditions of the analysis, and therefore find exquisite expression in the patient's interaction with the analyst, and in his responses to the events that influence this interaction. The core of genetic transferences lies in the effects upon present relatedness of pathogenic unconscious fantasies, memories, and introjects. In the analysis, these transference expressions include derivatives from each of the structural components—id, ego, and superego—as well as genetically precipitated introjects and influences from the patient's self-image. Genetic transference is basic to all other forms of transference, although the term should be reserved for those situations in which a transference expression can be directly and analytically traced to an earlier pathogenic relationship and experience. These transferences include relatively disguised derivatives of the relevant early experiences and the unconscious fantasies, needs, and conflicts generated by them, as well as the defenses mobilized by these earlier situations.

In determining the presence of a genetic transference reaction, the analyst must first establish and validate the existence of the transference component, identifying the specific transference object, the historical period from which the main unconscious fantasies and memories influencing the transference reaction are drawn, the specific traumatic experiences that occurred during this time, the pertinent defenses that were mobilized, and any additional contributions that may have stemmed from cumulative traumatic aspects of the relevant early childhood relationships. Since transference responses are overdetermined, the analyst must identify the central genetic transference component, as well as subsidiary ones.

A comprehensive interpretation of genetic transference should be offered from an adaptational-interactional framework, and requires a determination of the adaptive stimulus for a particular transference-based reaction, leading to an integrated comprehension of both the current precipitants and the genetic factors. Ultimately, in following the thread of the patient's associations within a specific current adaptive context, the analyst must definitively identify the fantasies and introjects on which the genetic transference reaction is based.

In all, genetic transference is intrapsychically founded, although it finds expression not only in the patient's verbalized derivatives, but also in the direct interaction with the analyst, leading to efforts to influence him and to evoke complementary responses and roles on his part. The central mechanisms for genetic transferences are also intrapsychic and are built around *displacements*, with subsidiary roles played by projection and introjection, depending on the particular form in which the transference reaction is expressed (see below).

Transference-Based Displacements from Current External Objects. A variant of classical or genetic transference involves those transference distortions that are based primarily on displacements onto the analyst from current external objects—persons in the patient's contemporary environment. In this form of transference, while there are always underlying genetic connections, and often additional projective and introjective mechanisms, the patient's distorted unconscious fantasies about, and wishes toward the analyst, and their derivatives, essentially result from displacements from current outside objects and the genetic sources are not immediately pertinent or available. Ultimately, of course, this type of transference can be traced to genetic transferences and to the other basic forms that will be described presently.

*Transference-Based Projections and Projective Iden-
tifications.* Transference-based projections and projective
identifications are distorting processes through which the
patient attributes to the analyst, or endeavors to place into
him, derivatives of his own inner structures and needs
(related to id, ego, or superego), aspects of his introjects, or
elements of his inner state or self-concept and self-
representation. Transference projections may be defined
as usually defensive efforts by the patient to deal with
intrapsychic conflicts, anxieties, and fantasies by attributing some aspect of himself to the analyst. It is essentially
an intrapsychic mechanism which may be communicated
directly or in derivative form to the analyst, but these
expressions are not primarily designed to influence the
analyst's inner state or to generate specific fantasies and
reactions within him—although they may do so secondarily. Their basic function is intrapsychic rather than
interactional.

This essentially intrapsychic type of projective effort
overlaps with and extends into projective identifications,
which are definitely interactional expressions of the
patient's projective defenses and needs. Such efforts are
designed not only to attribute to the analyst some aspect of
the patient's own pathological inner state, but characteristically represent endeavors to actually create the relevant
state within the analyst, so that the patient can then
manage these contents and needs outside of himself or
evoke proxy responses. An apt description of these
transference-based interactional efforts is that the patient
tries to place, put, or dump into the analyst his own
intrapsychic disturbances, fantasies, and introjects. The
concept of transference-based projective identification has
also been extended to include efforts to put into the
analyst good inner parts, and so long as these have

distorting elements, they may be included in the present classification.

For the sake of clarification, we may note that the term *identification* in projective identification is not used in the usual sense of the subject taking into himself attributes of the object, but refers instead to endeavors by the subject to evoke an identification in the object with an aspect of himself. It also alludes to the finding that the subject is still identified with the contents and inner state that he has placed into the object and that, in addition, these efforts at externalization are designed by the subject to manage his inner contents within another person—the external object or, specifically, the analyst in the case of transference-based projective identifications. Conceptual confusion might be lessened by using the term *interactional projection* for *projective identification*—a suggestion that I shall not further pursue here.

With this form of transference, an aspect that is actually pertinent to all transference communications comes to the fore. Unconsciously, the patient is motivated both by his defensive needs and by more positively toned wishes to experience and introject the analyst's constructive metabolism or working over of his transference communications—here, his projective identifications. This containing and handling by the analyst, especially when it is directed toward an appropriate and therapeutic interactional response and verbal interpretation, is critical to analytic outcome (see below).

Projections, then, are essentially intrapsychic processes that have secondary interactional effects that depend on the extent to which a projection and its inner consequences are communicated to the analyst. Projective identifications, on the other hand, entail basically interactional motives and processes, and always include some type of direct effort to put contents into the analyst for reasons that range from wishes for assistance with disturbing inner experiences, to efforts at inappropriate gratifications and attempts to harm and disrupt the functioning of the analyst.

Both transference projections and projective identifications may directly involve the analyst, although, like genetic transferences, they are at times displaced from the analyst onto others. While the contents that are projected onto or into the analyst or others are ultimately based on genetic experiences and their inner repercussions, these forms of transference expression are essentially responses to the patient's current adaptive tasks, and the related intrapsychic conflicts and fantasies, and involve efforts on various levels at externalization. While some writers have attempted to distinguish these projective mechanisms from other forms of externalization, it appears that these two basic processes encompass most efforts of the patient to disown, externalize, or project any aspect of his inner contents, structures, conflicts, anxieties and other affects, or self, and that further refinement is superfluous for present purposes.

The distinction between projection and projective identification is important both in regard to the form in which the patient's unconscious transference fantasies and needs are expressed, and the nature of the analyst's interpretation. In the main, transference-based projective identifications unfold within the bipersonal field and relationship between patient and analyst, and in identifying and validating their presence, the analyst relies largely on his comprehension of his own inner experiences, with additional clarification based on the derivatives conveyed in the patient's verbal associations. There need not, however, be a direct parallel between what the patient is experiencing and projectively identifying into the analyst, and what the analyst will experience under these circumstances. The latter has a full opportunity to process or metabolize the introjective identifications that are created within him through the patient's interactional projective efforts. In addition, the analyst's own intrapsychic needs, structures, introjects, and the like, are activated by the patient's projective identifications, and will influence their processing within him. His reaction may parallel the inner experience of the patient, may take a very different form, or may refute the contents entirely.

It is crucial, once the analyst has experienced, metabolized, and understood a projective identification, that he maintain or reestablish his separate identity and functioning, restoring those aspects of the self-object boundaries between himself and the analysand that were momentarily obliterated. He must also consciously identify and validate the nature of the projective identification that he has experienced, doing so from the patient's associations and from his own inner experience. In this way he metabolizes or processes the projective identification in an adaptive manner that eventually leads to an interpretation and to an appropriate interactional response. The pathological alternative has been termed *projective counteridentification*, in that the analyst unconsciously introjects the patient's pathological contents and responds with an unrecognized pathological reprojection of his own. This entails a therapeutic misalliance in which the analyst unconsciously accepts and utilizes the patient's pathological contents and mechanisms for his own neurotic needs. Clinically, this type of sequence may be identified by recognizing and evaluating the interactional implications of interpretive failures, mismanagements of the frame, pathological interactions, and the interactional efforts by the patient that have evoked them. This is done through the usual means of attending to the patient's associations and to the analyst's responses, with their interactional elements in mind.

Transference-based projective identifications may be expressed verbally in the patient's fantasies about the analyst or through the analysand's direct efforts to attribute specific qualities of his own to this therapist. This mechanism may also operate nonverbally, quite indirectly, and entirely within the framework of the patient's interaction with the analyst. Clinical observations indicate that transference-based and nontransference-based, distorted and valid, uses of projective identification constitute the single most important interactional process within the analytic situation—for both patient and analyst. This mechanism is prominent in patients with all types of psychopathology and at all levels of psychosexual and object-related development, and it is used by those who have intact ego- or self-boundaries and a strong capacity to relate, as well as those with blurred boundaries and disturbed object relationships. Thus, projective identification, as is true with any intrapsychic defense or mechanism, may be utilized in primitive or more mature forms and need not imply anything more than a selective loss of self-boundaries, although at times it may become massive enough to entail more lasting periods of such loss. In dealing with this interactional mechanism in the analytic situation, it is important first to explore and analyze its genetic implications, and second, to distinguish pathological and nonpathological forms.

Transference-Based Identifications and Introjective Identifications. Identification is essentially an intrapsychic mechanism through which the patient modifies some aspect of his self-representation or his intrapsychic structures on the basis of his conscious or, more often, unconscious needs and efforts to alter himself in accordance with his perceptions of another person—here, the analyst. Introjective identification is the companion mechanism to projective identification, and is an interactional process. Through it, the patient either accepts the projective identifications of another person, such as the analyst, or makes active efforts of his own to take into himself, contain, and metabolize contents or personality dimensions from another individual. While a projective identification is often experienced by the projector as depleting, introjective identification is characteristically felt to be enriching or filling, or an effort to deplete the object. While again on a continuum, identificatory processes have a less significant interactional component than does introjective identification, and they are not actively designed to capture contents and inner states from another individual to the same extent. By contrast, introjective identification is essentially interactional and is basically designed to incorporate aspects of the object and, as a rule, to process them and to communicate the effects of this metabolism.

In transference-based identifications, the patient unconsciously incorporates various aspects of the analyst's personality, functioning, inner state, intrapsychic structures, internal objects, unconscious fantasies, qualities or mode of interacting, and the like. Such processes are considered transference-related when they are based on or lead to distorted perceptions of and reactions to the analyst, or when they are linked to specific, pathological, intrapsychic fantasies and introjects within the patient. Therefore, to the extent that the patient's identifications with the analyst are distorting, defensive, or inappropriately gratifying, they are a facet of transference.

When the patient, for neurotic and inappropriate motives and needs, accepts the analyst's projections and projective identifications into himself, he is using transference-based introjective identifications. In his processing of these incorporated contents—pathological or nonpathological—he is not, however, limited to parallel experiences and inner states. He may elaborate these introjective identifications according to his own needs, further distort them, or defend himself against them and reject them, doing so in a complex interaction with the analyst that includes many possible outcomes.

This category of identificatory and introjective transference-based mechanisms includes the patient's neurotically motivated empathic responses to the analyst's introjects, inner structures and needs, and his inappropriate identifications with the analyst's past and present objects. These mechanisms may be the basis for therapeutic misalliances, pathological interactions, shared defenses, and the gratification of neurotic needs. Among the most important introjective identifications of the analyst by the analysand are those that involve the former's psychopathology as reflected in his inappropriate interventions and mismanagements of the framework. They are generated by both transference-based and nontransference-based motives: the analysand will incorporate the sick parts of the analyst and, as a rule, both exploit the introjection for neurotic gain (the transference component) and offer valid curative efforts (the nontransference component).

These, then, are the basic sources of transference distortions in the patient's relationship with the analyst. Perhaps the most fundamental division pertains to genetic and interactional transferences. Their analysis provides the most viable means of understanding and resolving the patient's emotional problems, for they bear a significant relationship to the unconscious fantasies, memories, and introjects that are the basis for the patient's psychopathology. In essence, the distorting forces that produce transference reactions are intimately bound with those that create neurotic and more severe symptoms and characterological disturbances. While the underlying pathogenic constellations influence all of the patient's relationships and interactions, and therefore find expression in outside contacts as well as in those with the analyst, the special conditions of the patient's investment in the analytic relationship and of the nature of the bipersonal therapeutic field foster their expression and render the analysis of transference constellations the most effective means of affording the patient adaptive, inner structural change. This analytic work is also enhanced because the analyst is in an especially opportune position to validate his identification of the distorting and pathological components of the patient's communications, and to distinguish them from more realistic aspects. There is room for analytic work in both areas—within and outside the analytic relationship—depending on the primary adaptive context facing the patient at a given moment. The most effective type of analytic work stems from a balanced approach that considers both spheres, and that concentrates on the transference aspects primarily because, at most times, they are most pertinent to the patient's intrapsychic anxieties and conflicts. This holds true equally in analysis and in therapy, within the limits imposed by the conditions of the latter. Having established this fundamental classification of transference in terms of the basic and prevailing intrapsychic and interactional mechanisms, let us now examine its other main dimensions.

The Forms of
Transference Expression

At the core of a transference distortion is an unconscious fantasy or introject within the patient and, interactionally, the operation of projective and introjective identification. These intrapsychic and interactional processes are expressed in conscious and behavioral ways, grossly or subtly, directly with the analyst and in outside relationships; they constitute the forms of transference expression, an element of which is contained in every communication from the patient to the analyst. Considerable confusion has arisen because of the failure clinically to distinguish unconsicous transference fantasies and interactional mechanisms, from their surface manifestations. Let us now examine the expressions of transference.

Transference as Conscious Fantasy. It is important conceptually to recognize that conscious fantasies about the analyst—or others through displacement—are *derivatives* of unconsious fantasies and mechanisms. They may be relatively defended and disguised representations, or may be more direct expressions of their unconscious counterparts. The analyst should not restrict himself to the manifest content of such fantasies, but must analyze their elements in terms of their adaptive contexts and the patient's associations in order to arrive at their latent content, the intrapsychic and interactional mechanisms involved, and the actual underlying sources of the transference distortions. Technically, it behooves the analyst to maintain an ear for transference components in every conscious fantasy expressed by the patient; these may be heavily disguised—distant derivatives, or relatively undisguised—close derivatives.

Considerable conceptual confusion has stemmed from the restriction of the term *transference* to conscious fantasies about the analyst. As a result, the concepts of resistance and of defenses against transference expressions have generally been tied to efforts to defend against directly conscious fantasies about the analyst, and have not been related to the entire range of manifestations of unconscious transference fantasies. Patients who have been described as resisting or denying "the transference" are actually, as a rule, simply not communicating noticeable, analyzable conscious fantasies about the analyst. In general, such analysands express their unconscious transference fantasies in other forms or have transference constellations in which the defensive elements are especially prominent.

These comments have a bearing on the broader problem of the characteristic form or patterning of the patient's transference constellation, an aspect that is largely determined by factors within the analysand, though definitively influenced by the analyst. Empirical evidence indicates, as I have noted, that the relationship that the patient develops with the analyst is unique and important—a powerful stimulus for unconscious fantasies, and projective and introjective processes. The specific manner in which the patient manages these thrusts toward transference expression characterizes his transference syndrome. Each patient has a preference for given forms of transference expression, defense, and interaction. This depends on the entire gamut of intrapsychic factors, and to a lesser extent on the analyst and the nature of the bipersonal field. Intrapsychically, the balance between the intensity of the instinctual drives, superego promptings, and a variety of ego capacities play an especially important role. On another level, the primary mode of communication, such as the use of verbalized derivatives or a preference for interactional efforts, itself based on a variety of factors, is also important.

The expression of unconscious transference fantasies through conscious fantasies about the analyst may be a preferred mode of expression in patients who tend to communicate through fantasy and verbalization, and are less likely to displace these fantasies onto others. This mode may reflect a relative flexibility and maturity of defensive operations when these fantasies are well controlled and modulated, and appear in relatively analyzable form; or it may reflect brittle and impaired defenses when this material is blatant, poorly managed and modulated, and difficult to analyze—for example, the so-called instinctualized or erotized transferences. The relative absence of such conscious fantasies may reflect a preference for interactional expressions of unconscious transference fantasies and introjects through such behaviors as "acting out" and acting in, the evocation of roles and proxies, and the use of projective and introjective identifications. It may also reflect a markedly defense-laden unconscious transference constellation and the use of secondary defenses against the emergence of direct expressions of the relevant unconscious transference fantasies in the relationship with the analyst.

Acting Out or Living Out. A common and well-known form of transference expression is that of acting or living out, which, in its narrowest definition, is the enactment of unconscious transference fantasies and memories in the relationship with the analyst, and secondarily, in situations that are external to the analytic setting. These terms generally have been used to allude to gross behaviors of the patient, including certain types of symptomatic actions, as well as more extended and elaborate dramas that are lived out rather than consciously remembered or verbally communicated. More recently, the basic concept has been somewhat broadened to include efforts at reenactment in which the patient intends for the analyst to adopt a role in keeping with the patient's unconscious transference fantasies and therefore, with the behaviors of past pathogenic figures.

Historically, because there was a tendency to stress the communication of unconscious transference fantasies through verbalized derivatives—as conscious fantasies and memories—there was an accompanying trend toward considering living out and efforts at reenactment either as resistances or as less analytically valuable means of communicating transference expressions. More recently, there has been a more balanced perspective which recognizes living out and efforts at reenactment as valid and important ways of communicating and expressing unconscious transference fantasies. While their special potential for disruptive resistances is recognized, analytic resolution of these behaviors in which their present and past meanings are identified and worked through has been established as an important means of attaining valid insights. It is now also understood that this form of transference expression is universal and will occur in all analyses, although some types of patients are particularly prone to its use.

The identification of the transference components in living out and efforts at reenactment depends on: the recognition of the adaptive context for the patient's behaviors, the nonparticipation of the analyst which would otherwise generate a sector of misalliance and render him unable to intervene interpretively, the detection of the derivatives of the unconscious transference fantasies embedded in the particular behavior, and their interpretation and working through. The analyst must constantly monitor for transference expressions all behaviors of the patient, and all pressures on himself to behave or react in noninterpretive ways. It is also crucial that he distinguish between those of the patient's behaviors that are largely pathological and those that are adaptive, leaving room for the patient's autonomy and his need for valid, experimental trial action.

Transference as Interaction with the Analyst. This form of transference expression overlaps with the previous category—acting out-living out—but deserves separate consideration. It is perhaps the most pervasive means of transference communication, and it has many subspecies. It includes all of the patient's projective and introjective identifications that take place within the relationship with the analyst, and all gross efforts at living out (see above), as well as far more subtle endeavors to reenact and to involve the analyst in some type of nontherapeutic interaction. It pertains to a realm the analyst must continually monitor, one that goes beyond the contents of the patient's verbal associations, and that especially mandates the investigation of interactional processes and effects that the patient is trying to create in the analyst through such diverse means as the manner in which he associates, the gaps in these associations, his behaviors, and his overall style of communicating.

This is a difficult category of transference manifestations to describe without extensive clinical examples, and its comprehension depends on the analyst's sensitivity to such expressions—especially their more subtle forms. Thus, one context for the analyst's listening and experiencing centers on the question of what it is that the patient is trying to do to the analyst—put into him, stir up in him, have him react, seduce, attack, and the like. The analyst's subjective sensitivities, the validity of which rely on his self-knowledge, are an important guide; so is a study of the patient's associations for latent content related to his unconscious awareness of the interactional pressures and actualities that he is creating.

For example, a patient whose associations show virtually no analyzable derivatives of his unconscious fantasies may be unconsciously attempting to effect an interaction with the analyst in which the latter is frustrated, defeated, enraged, or enticed to attack. Interactionally, the patient may be attempting to treat the analyst in a particular manner or to create an interactional void, thereby gratifying directly in the relationship certain unconscious transference fantasies and needs. Here, the transference derivatives are expressed not so much in the manifest and latent content of the patient's associations, as in what the patient is doing, how he is treating the analyst, and in the responses and roles that he is trying to evoke. He may be subtly or grossly seductive or provocative, and may attempt in a variety of ways to create distance from or excessive closeness to the analyst, or to have him respond inappropriately. Eventually, the verbalized material will usually contain derivatives of the patient's own unconscious perceptions of his transference-based behaviors, or of the fantasied expressions of these interactional efforts. In dealing with them analytically, it is essential that the analyst not respond according to the patient's inappropriate needs and thereby create a sector of misalliance. Rather, he must experience these evocations in a controlled or signal manner, carefully validate his impressions and formulations, and ultimately react interpretively.

Interactional transference manifestations often over-shadow the manifest and latent content of the patient's verbalized associations. These associations may actually be communicated primarily for interactional needs rather than cognitive exploration, and such actualities must be dealt with before any meaningful work with the content of the material can be undertaken. Since these interactional endeavors are in the service of important transference gratifications and resistances, and are often designed to reinforce and confirm the patient's neurosis, a restrictive focus on content at such times will lead to sectors of misalliance and stalemate. All deviant or unusual feelings within the analyst—frustration, anger, stimulation, confusion, self-satisfaction, self-aggrandizement, and the like—call for an investigation of the interactional efforts of the patient. In all, then, this form of interactive transference manifestation entails efforts by the patient to have the analyst behave or experience in ways that are comparable to significant transference objects, and to gratify unconscious transference wishes and defenses.

Projective and introjective identification have already been discussed in the section on basic transference mechanisms; they constitute another major form of interactional transference expression. Here, transference is expressed in direct, usually unconscious, interactional efforts with the analyst, including endeavors to put contents, affects, and the like into him for safekeeping, harm, or other processing, to evoke responsive proxies, and to incorporate from him responsive contents, functions, and the like.

This common form of transference expression is prompted by many motives, including the patient's reactions to the analyst's projective identifications, his pathological wishes to cure or merge with the analyst, and his unconscious wishes to both modify and maintain his neuroses. To further illustrate: a given patient may associate in a rambling, confused, and excited manner. The content of his associations may not prove illuminating until organized around the interactional efforts so contained. Such associations may reflect unconscious wishes to create in the analyst the state of confusion and frustration experienced by the patient, or may be efforts to put into the analyst a hostile introject (there need not be a direct parallel between the manifest vehicle of a projective identification and the underlying desired interactional effects). By utilizing his subjective awareness of the influence of the patient's communications, and by identifying the adaptive context, the analyst is in a position to understand that the patient is attempting to projectively identify into him his own inner state of confusion and overexcitement, and, more dynamically, aspects of his harsh superego and poor ego controls. The analyst may momentarily feel confused and guilty over not being able to understand and help the patient, and if these inner disturbances are not maintained at a signal level, his interventions will reflect their disruptive impact and constitute projective counteridentifications in which the analyst unconsciously attempts to reproject the inner disequilibrium that the patient had placed into him; this is a failure in metabolizing and in understanding. Similarly, the analyst may react with counterhostilities, or with efforts to seduce or placate the patient on some level, thereby maladaptively processing the projective identification in still another nontherapeutic way. Thus, the analyst may experience aspects of the contents, fantasies, and inner state that the patient is attempting to place into him; he may then process them in keeping with his own pathological inner needs, responding predominantly on the basis of his own idiosyncratic reactions. However, by maintaining these responses as signals and by resorting to his understanding of himself and his own tendencies in responding to projective identifications, the analyst will be consciously able to recognize what the patient is attempting to place into him.

Then, turning to the patient's verbal associations for manifest and especially latent content, and to the adaptive context that has set off the sequence, he can both validate the nature of the analysand's interactional efforts and appropriately interpret them within an adaptational-interactional framework. Such an intervention would provide the patient not only with cognitive insight, but with an implicit opportunity to identify with and introject an object—the analyst—who is able to constructively manage projective identifications and potentially disruptive inner states. Such an outcome stands in contrast to the negative introjective identifications and the disruptive effects that follow from the therapist's countertransference-based responsive, pathological, projective identifications, which largely serve to confirm the patient's inner pathology and his distorted unconscious transference fantasies, and may even intensify them.

This is a cumbersome general description, but I believe it clarifies ways in which the patient's style and manner of associating and behaving convey interactional, transference-based wishes, defenses, and efforts to generate inner states and roles within the analyst. Such endeavors have been relatively neglected in the classical psychoanalytic literature, while they have been overemphasized in Kleinian writings, to the relative disregard of other types of transference expression. Essential to understanding this form of transference is the recognition that there are two basic dimensions to all transference reactions, the intrapsychic and the interactional, and that these two spheres are involved in an extensive interplay. A given unconscious transference fantasy or introject therefore has a variety of intrapsychic repercussions, may evoke various interactional efforts and effects, and will be influenced, in turn, by the behaviors and responses of others—especially the analyst. The concept of the analysis of transference must therefore be broadened to include both spheres.

Finally, it is in the area of interactional transference expressions that we come most clearly to recognize that the analyst actually has a dual task: that of managing his responses to the patient's behaviors and communications, and that of interpreting their unconscious meanings and implications. Control of countertransference-based reactions and counterresponses is a prerequisite for the comprehension of the patient's transference fantasies and for effective interpretations, since a participating pathological response will confirm behaviorally the patient's unconscious fantasy, create a negative image of the analyst, and preclude the positive modifying effects of the analyst's verbal interventions. It is here that it becomes crucial that the analyst not gratify the patient's transference wishes, not provide extratherapeutic gratifications, and properly maintain the frame. The analyst is inevitably under consistent pressures from the patient—and from within himself to some extent—to actualize his unconscious transference fantasies and introjects in the direct analytic interaction; this is an area that merits consistent monitoring, management, and interpretation.

Transference as Belief, Intention, Distorted Perception, Delusion, and Hallucination. Overlapping with the previous categories are a variety of transference forms that include delusional beliefs, hallucinatory experiences, inappropriate, direct, conscious intentions toward the analyst, and grossly distorted impressions and contentions. These experiences may occur in the relationship with the analyst or with others, and are manifested in thought and behavior, especially in the interaction with the analyst. In general, these expressions reflect two types of psychopathology which, in the extreme, may be of psychotic proportions. First, they tend to reflect derivatives of extremely primitive instinctual-drive expressions and similarly archaic superego pressures. They also involve a variety of impairments in ego functions—for example, reality testing, relating to reality, judgment, controls, and the general management of one's impulses—and the predominant use of primitive defensive operations. Second, they reflect failures in the manner in which the patient experiences, manages, and gains distance from his transference impulses.

The basis for a transference expression—an amalgam of id, ego, superego, and the influence of external realities—is an unconscious, intrapsychic compromise. But once a derivative of this inner configuration has been actualized and experienced by the patient, he attempts to manage it by mobilizing a variety of ego functions: gaining a perspective on the nature of his impulse, measuring it against the realities of the analytic relationship (it is of course crucial that these realities not correspond to his inner distortions), and maintaining himself at some distance from the impulse, lest he become embedded in it to the extent of making it ego-syntonic and therefore endeavoring to live it out in some gross form. When the instinctual-drive pressures are too intense or too primitive, superego contribution too archaic and pressing, initial ego defense relatively primitive and impaired, and controls poor, the patient has an extremely difficult secondary task of mobilizing adequate defenses and other ego operations to deal with his transference reaction which, in itself, tends under these conditions to be especially intense, commanding action and gratification. Particularly when these secondary defenses are impaired or fail, the patient loses distance from the derivative expressions of his unconscious transference fantasies and becomes rather blindly identified with them, expressing them in forms that seek immediate discharge or that occur as near-delusional or delusional beliefs and intentions reflecting a loss of perspective on the psychoanalytic relationship.

The analyst, however, by the manner in which he maintains the relationship and the framework, and intervenes or fails to intervene, makes his own crucial contribution to these more disturbed transference expressions. If he in any way blurs the ground rules and boundaries of the analytic relationship, or if his unconscious and conscious intentions with the patient are unclear, or if he resorts to pathological interactional mechanisms, the patient's unconscious perceptions and introjections of these impairments will contribute to and reinforce his own difficulties in managing his transference responses. Often, an analyst who unnecessarily modifies the frame is blind to the unconscious meanings and communications contained in his deviation, with respect both to their content and how they reflect his own unconscious difficulties. Similarly, the analyst's errors in intervening convey a variety of pathological unconscious fantasies, express his countertransference-based efforts at projective identification into the patient of his own sick contents, and present an image of an unmanaging analyst.

The patient will be quite sensitive to the many implications of these errors in technique, so that his own intentions vis-à-vis the analyst, which appear to the latter inappropriate or transference-based, actually may have received an important contribution or impetus from the analyst himself; in fact, at times such a respnse may be quite appropriate in light of the behaviors and unconscious communications from the analyst. However, it is the patient's responsibility, despite provocation from the analyst, to manage his responses and to control, modulate, and maintain a perspective on his transference expressions. The resultant situation is, as always, a compromise of intrapsychic factors within the patient and analyst, and of their shared interaction and communications.

When the analysand's behavior is primarily distorted and not in keeping with the conscious and unconscious communications from the analyst, it is essentially transference-based; on the other hand, if his reactions are appropriate to unconscious facets of the analyst's behaviors, these responses are primarily reality-based, with secondary genetic and transference components. Failure to establish these distinctions will further impair the patient's testing of inner and outer reality, his management of his transference expressions, the therapeutic alliance, and the basic relationship with the analyst.

This category of transference includes the instinctualized transferences, as represented by the erotized and aggressified transference reactions. In these situations, the patient shows direct wishes to become sexually involved with the analyst, or to attack him verbally or physically. These transference responses are characterized by the intensity of the patient's intentions, by their relative lack of justification in light of the analyst's own behaviors and communications, and by the features already described in general for this group of transference expressions. At the least, they reflect a variety of intrapsychic disturbances and impairments in ego functions, and may in extreme form reflect psychotic pathology (see also below).

Transference as Symptom. The final major form through which unconscious transference fantasies and introjects are expressed is that of symptoms within the patient. These may include the usual psychological symptom complexes such as anxiety, obsessions, and phobias. Such somatic components as psychosomatic and conversion symptoms may be present and they may be of neurotic, borderline, or psychotic proportions. Identifying them as transference-based depends upon understanding the adaptive context that evoked their occurrence, and upon evaluating the patient's associations and behaviors to detect the underlying unconscious transference fantasies and interactional efforts. It is important here, too, to be aware of any possible contributions from the analyst that evoke such symptomatic responses—that is, help to create interactional syndromes—although ultimately the analytic goal is intrapsychically to modify both the underlying fantasies and the patient's propensity toward symptomatic or somatic expression.

The Diagnostic Classification of Transference Reactions

We may also consider the types of transference in terms of clinical diagnostic entities, a classification that overlaps with the forms described above. Thus, we may identify hysterical or obsessive transference manifestations and other neurotic forms, and borderline, psychotic, or narcissistic transferences. It is possible to develop other diagnostic classifications, such as those based on character structure or personality patterns—an effort that will not be pursued here.

The "Transference Illusion"

The delineation of analyzable forms of transference brings up the question of the patient's capacity to maintain the so-called transference illusion. These "as if" qualities have been viewed as a distinguishing hallmark of the usual transference manifestations, differentiating them from experiences that occur in the course of daily life outside the analytic relationship. The illusion concept argues that the patient is reacting to the analyst primarily in terms of past relationships rather than his immediate present one and that, while subjectively experienced as real, his feelings toward the analyst will be maintained with a perspective that recognizes their inappropriate qualities. At issue is the distinction between illusion and reality, and the potential use of the illusion concept by the analyst to defensively deny the appropriateness of his patient's feelings and his own contribution in evoking them.

The concept has valid elements in attributing to transference reactions a special type of human response that occurs in a properly established and managed analytic setting. It would appear, however, that this unique quality does not stem primarily from the genetic contributions to transference distortions: these may be present in an outside relationship, but we do not then label the patient's feelings and fantasies as illusional unless certain additional conditions are met. It is rather the analytic relationship itself, and the framework which operates to maintain a patient-analyst relationship geared toward the analytic cure of the patient, that provides the two basic components of the illusion effect: first, that certain experiences of the patient primarily reflect his own inner needs and defenses, and not the external conditions of the relationship with the analyst, no matter how intensely the patient experiences them in such terms; and second, that the expression of these inner needs and defenses will not knowingly be directly gratified by either participant. In such a setting, the communications of the patient, no matter how intensely he wishes to include their gratification, are treated as derivatives of his intrapsychic conflicts and fantasies, and are analyzed.

Critical for the transference illusion, then, is a stable and consistently managed framework, the unswerving interpretive efforts and noninvolvement of the analyst—so far as gratifying the patient's neurotic needs or responding to them in a manner that confirms their inner basis and reinforces their reality—and certain basic capacities and perspectives within the analysand. These latter depend first upon his conscious and unconscious perceptions of the analyst, and on various identifications with and introjections of the analyst's capacity to maintain controls and perspective; and second, they depend upon the patient's own abilities to manage his transference derivatives (maintain a clear understanding of the nature of the analytic relationship), to accept the established boundaries, to recognize the unlikelihood of direct gratification, to become aware of the distorted aspects and genetic roots of his inappropriate needs and reactions, and to maintain an adequate distance from his inner transference stirrings (see above). The adequate use of a number of complex ego functions is essential, especially at moments when the patient experiences seemingly intense, realistic feelings and wishes toward the analyst. On some level he must have the capability to recognize that other factors are present, and that there are both realistic and unrealistic components to his response. The net outcome may be an ego-syntonic acceptance of transference-based wishes as valid and likely to be gratified, which in the absence of contributions from the analyst reflects significant intrapsychic pathology; or the patient may be able to maintain an implicit recognition that his transference-based wishes are unlikely to be gratified, are derived from inner and distorting sources, and are essentially invalid in the analytic relationship (the maintenance of spheres of relatively autonomous ego functioning in the presence of areas of ego disturbance). The analyst's efforts to safeguard the transference through maintenance of the frame and interpretive responses serve to reinforce those ego functions that help the patient with this perspective.

The Predominant Function of the Transference Expression

Undoubtedly other groupings of transference could be made, but I shall close this section on the classification of transference by comparing its function as the expression of resistances with that of conveying unconscious memories and fantasies. Here again, the two intermingle, although separate description clarifies the two basic functions of transference and the adaptational-interactional form that its communication may take.

Certain expressions of unconscious transference fantasies operate primarily as resistances in the interaction with the analyst: they are manifestations of derivatives of unconscious fantasies in which the defensive elements are central, or which for the moment serve the defenses of the analysand and the disruption of the analytic work. When a particularly threatening unconscious transference fantasy has been stirred up by some adaptive context, the patient's defenses are mobilized and may lead to living out or efforts at reenactment, thereby gratifying the fantasy directly with the analyst or in an outside relationship so that the underlying derivatives and anxieties are repressed or otherwise defended against. As alternatives, the patient may mobilize a projective identification through which he attempts to place the contents and affects of the unconscious transference fantasy into the analyst, or he may avail himself of a more simplified projective mechanism in which he experiences a number of distortions in his perceptions, defensively and intrapsychically attributing to the analyst aspects of his own underlying disturbing transference fantasy. All such efforts are designed in part to create obstacles to insightful analytic work and to the search for intrapsychically-based, adaptive structural change; in essence, they serve the resistances of the analysand. Nonetheless, it is evident that such defensively dominated fantasies and their derivatives simultaneously reveal a great deal about the nature of the underlying fantasies that are being defended against, and about the patient's defensive propensities in general—that is, they can also serve the positive goals of analysis.

By contrast, those derivatives of unconscious transference fantasies that primarily express and reveal core unconscious memories, fantasies, introjects, and conflicts may be viewed as the ideal model of the revealing, unconscious transference constellation. Consistent analytic work with the primarily defensive transference components will ultimately lead to these core fantasies, to which they are related and which, in turn, are the primary basis for the patient's neurotic symptoms and characterological disturbances. With the interpretation and working through of these core fantasies, one finds that they too, in addition to their communicative functions, are used for defense-resistance, a function usually revealed through subsequent analytic work: primarily revealing transference constellations secondarily serve as significant resistances to other levels of material. Both the intimate connection between defensive and revealing transference constellations and the fluctuation between defensiveness and revelation is characteristic of all viable analytic work.

It becomes clear that the analyst has to experience and monitor not only a wide range of communications and interactional efforts by the patient, but he must also endeavor to ascertain multiple meanings and implications. These tasks form but one group of reasons why total mastery of the analytic relationship and interaction can be at best a hypothetical ideal toward which every analyst strives, with the humble recognition of its elusiveness. On the other hand, despite the enormity of this task, it is possible to reach a significant level of mastery, to produce effective analytic work, and to be capable of recognizing and modifying inevitable difficulties.

The Detection of
Unconscious Transference Fantasies

Many believe that the presence of a transference reaction is, clinically speaking, self-evident to the experienced psychoanalyst. There is much evidence, however, that the study of this crucial empirical determination actually constitutes one of the most significant lacunae in the psychoanalytic literature on the patient-analyst relationship. Without the establishment of clear-cut clinical criteria and their validation, there can be no comprehensive and unchallenged literature on this subject. Because of inevitable biases regarding such assessments within the therapist, these efforts require careful personal and general scrutiny.

Establishing the Adaptive Context. Since the essence of a transference expression is an unconscious intrapsychic fantasy or introject that distorts the patient's perceptions of and interaction with the analyst or his representative, it is necessary first to establish the presence of such a distortion, distinguishing it from essentially realistic reactions. Such efforts require that the analyst have a sound grasp of inner and outer reality as it pertains both to himself and to the patient, constantly monitor this dimension, and consistently validate his conclusions. Perhaps the first step in this process is to identify the "day residue" or adaptive stimulus for the patient's associations and behaviors. That is, the analyst assesses the implications and potential of the reality precipitants for the patient's adaptive efforts. To do this, the analyst must establish the unconscious meanings of both his own and the patient's behaviors and communications, and determine their general implications and specific unconscious relevance for the analysand. This especially requires that he ascertain the nature of his interventions and whether he has made them in a neutral manner or has erred or modified the frame in this regard or any other. This is a complex assessment process that involves not simply identifying gross stimuli and their manifest content, but attending to the entire realm of their latent implications, including those that are interactional.

Clues to the Appropriateness of the Patient's Reactions. In tracing the patient's responses to an adaptive stimulus relevant to the analytic relationship, the analyst searches for clues to the extent to which the patient's wish, perception, or behavior is appropriate to the conditions of the analytic setting and to the analyst's own behaviors, and therefore not primarily transference-based; or else how it is distorted and inappropriate vis-à-vis these conditions, and therefore primarily transference-based. In this assessment, he draws on the patient's communications and his own subjective experiences.

The analyst may begin by assessing how the analysand's direct comments illuminate his perceptions of an intervention or of an aspect of the management of the framework. The patient's additional associations may be in keeping with this assessment, or may be at odds with it. The entire constellation is compared with the analyst's own evaluation of his intervention, and undertaken with an openness that permits revision based on the patient's conscious and unconscious communications. All divergences from the analyst's carefully determined and validated assessment of the realities of the situation, and all inconsistencies within the various levels and components of the analysand's response, are signs of distortion and transference.

The analyst's task, however, is quite complicated and he cannot rely on a single criterion or level of exploration; clearly his evaluation is founded on his capacity to conceive and test reality, using this as the main standard with which he assesses the appropriateness of the patient's responses. Because of the possibility of strong personal bias, all such assessments must be validated by the subsequent associations of the patient and through additional clues from the analyst's subjective experiences and efforts at reconsideration. These endeavors should include a continuous investigation of the patient's unconscious and implicit communications for his perceptions and introjections of the analyst's behaviors and attitudes, and his consequent responses. The patient's great unconscious sensitivity to the analyst's inner life, stance, and interventions is an important resource that has been relatively neglected in the literature.

More broadly, the analyst can avail himself of the analysand's conscious and unconscious efforts to validate his own perceptions of and reactions to the analyst's behaviors. While there can be distorted unconscious perceptions, this aspect of the patient's associations is generally founded in veridical unconscious perceptions. The analyst must determine the degree to which the patient's introjective identifications reflect the analyst's implict and explicit behaviors and communications, and the extent to which they contain the patient's elaborations and distortions of what has been projectively identified into him.

In a typical sequence, there will be an adaptive context relevant to the analytic relationship, a conscious or unconscious response by the analysand which is assessed as primarily transference- or nontransference-based and subsequent associations that inherently reflect the patient's sense of the appropriateness of his reaction and its underlying basis. This may include direct references to the analyst, though at times the entire communication unfolds through various displacements by the patient onto others, especially himself. Constant assessment and reassessment is essential for the analyst, and use of the patient's communications is supplemented by use of his own inner responsiveness.

The analyst is continuously scrutinizing his own subjective feelings, fantasies, cognitive formulations, evaluations, and other aspects of his inner experiences for data relevant to his assessment of the patient's reactions. He will utilize all available tools, applying cognitive efforts at understanding and assessing reality, his empathic responses, identifications with the patient's internal and external objects, and broad knowledge of himself and of his own momentary inner stirrings. He must be aware of his own tendencies to distort or misperceive, his biases and vulnerabilities, blind spots, and defensive needs in the analytic relationship, especially those propensities that might prompt him, defensively or otherwise, to identify a reaction of the patient as transference-based when it is not. It is to be stressed that the analyst's assessment of a given communication or behavior in this regard is by no means simply intellectual or unilateral, but is actually a dynamic and interactional process—a product of the bipersonal field and subjected to its influences, including those derived from the patient and especially those stemming from the intrapsychic processes of the analyst.

It is beyond the scope of this outline to describe the unconscious conflicts and motives that could distort the analyst's assessment of the transference components in the patient's behavior (see chapter 4). Any unresolved intrapsychic conflict and neurotically defensive and gratifying needs that prevail in the relationship with the patient can be at work. Here, I wish to stress the constant interplay between the patient's communications and the analyst's subjective reactions, and the repeated alternation between himself and the patient as sources of data for generating and validating these assessments. These evaluations are truly a product of the bipersonal field in both their formulation and validation; unconsciously and at times consciously, the patient will endeavor to foster or impede these efforts by the analyst. As always, failures at validation must prompt both reassessment and a consideration of possible countertransference-based contributions to an evaluative error.

Finally, in establishing the realistic and fantasied components of his interaction with the patient, the analyst must be especially sensitive to the presence of projective and introjective identifications from the patient and himself, since these mechanisms are the most common basis for interactional transference distortions and for the interactional influences on erroneous assessments of the transference component by the analyst. In this sphere, mislabeling a communication from the patient as a transference expression initially may be a projection of an aspect of the analyst's countertransference onto the patient, and an intervention based on such an incorrect evaluation constitutes an effort to put into the patient aspects of the analyst's own inner disturbed state and fantasies—in order to extrude them, manage them outside himself, evoke proxies from the patient, and the like. Similarly, under the influence of the patient's pathological projective identifications, failures to properly metabolize the resultant introjective identification will also lead to misconceptions of the patient's reactions by the analyst. Interactionally, projective and introjective identifications may also influence the validating process, creating the possibility of interactionally shared mistakes in assessment, split-off and denied bastions, and sectors of misalliance. Repeated application of the validating process is an essential measure for safeguarding these determinations and for correcting inevitable errors.

Establishing and Interpreting the Basis for the Transference Manifestation. If the analyst is correct in his assessment that a given behavior or communication from the patient is in some way inappropriate and transference-based, the previous and subsequent material from the patient, and his own subjective evaluation, should enable him to delineate the genetic and interactional basis of the underlying unconscious transference fantasies and introjects. Definitive validation, however, comes after an interpretation based on such a formulation is offered and a further confirmatory response emerges from the patient—at times supplemented by further realizations by the analyst himself. Full clarification is often not possible in a single session, but definitive indicators of confirmation should appear rather quickly as a rule. The entire constellation of the patient's response must be assessed, since the appearance of relevant genetic material is in itself not generally a conclusive factor (nontransference-based reactions to the analyst's errors also have their genetic underpinnings). This step is largely a matter of the "fit" of the different aspects of the material, the uniqueness of the confirmatory communications, the presence of both cognitive and identificatory validation, and of the general fullness of the validating responses (see chapter 1).

The analyst's interventions—both maintaining or securing the frame and interpreting—most specifically activate within the analytic field his conception of the unconscious fantasies and processes within the analysand that are the source of immediate distortions of the analytic relationship, and offer the most singular moments for insight and verification. Within the bipersonal field, these efforts are most effective when applied not only to the manifest and latent content of the patient's associations and actions, but also to the implicit meanings of his interactions with the analyst. In this latter sphere, as I have noted, accurate assessment is especially difficult: there is a major nonverbal component and the analyst himself is involved in the interaction with the patient. It requires considerable sensitivity to the conscious and unconscious qualities and implications of the interaction and to the multiple, implicit and explicit meanings of the analyst's interventions.

A full appreciation of the complexities and difficulties in validly identifying the patient's transference responses creates an analytic climate in which the analyst will not automatically treat his patient's reactions as primarily transference, but will be open to recognize the many nontransference components of the patient's wishes, perceptions, and reactions. Such a perspective is enriching as well for the analyst, who comes to appreciate that correct interventions and proper management of the framework produce many inevitable hurts and that the maintenance of his own neutrality, anonymity, and central devotion to the analytic needs of the patient is a most trying task in which he may easily falter—and, if sensitive, readily integrate and recover. There is no doubt that the analyst's responsibilities become far more onerous and emotionally demanding when he is engaged in a continuous search for valid and distorted elements in the patient's communications, as compared to the situation in which the concept of transference is taken for granted and the patient's associations are viewed, with relatively few exceptions, as inappropriate. The latter stance fosters the analyst's unconscious use of the transference concept for defensive and self-gratifying needs, especially where his own errors and problems, and the patient's perceptions of them, are concerned. Nonetheless, the rewards for both himself and especially for his analysand that come from a sensitivity to these difficult distinctions offer ample compensation.

The Nontransference Components

The nontransference elements of the patient's relationship and interaction with the analyst include all wishes, perceptions, reactions, and interactional processes that are based on nondistorted cognitive assessments and inner needs, whether conscious or unconscious. These responses are realistic and appropriate to the conditions of the relationship and the bipersonal field, and they may be reflected directly in the interaction with or communications about the analyst, or through displacements. They are predominantly motivated by the patient's wishes for appropriate gratifications within the analytic relationship—reasonable expectations of understanding and symptom alleviation—and they entail valid adaptive reactions to the analytic setting or to the analyst's interventions.

Nontransference elements are not to be equated with the patient's conscious reactions or with the manifest content of his associations and behaviors, since they constitute a sphere which includes accurate unconscious perceptions, nonpathological unconscious fantasies and introjects, appropriate defenses, nonpathological superego expressions, and the gratification of appropriate, nonneurotic, instinctual-drive derivatives. It also encompasses nonpathological utilization of projective and introjective identifications in the interaction with the analyst. These aspects are not well described by the term *real relationship*, which implies a series of distinct and different relationships between the analysand and his analyst, nor are they identical to the therapeutic alliance, which is an interactional concept that derives from many nontransference elements within the patient, but also contains transference-based dimensions as well.

Nontransference reactions may be at times subsequently processed with in the patient in keeping with transference-based, distorting, pathogenic needs, but this is by no means their only fate; the patient is quite capable of maintaining segments of nonconflicted functioning, needing, perceiving, reacting, and relating in his interaction with the analyst. The basic components of nontransference-based reactions may be classified to some extent in a manner that parallels the study of the transference component, and I shall briefly develop their main qualities.

Matrix and Reactive Nontransference Elements

Matrix Nontransference. A wide range of nonconflicted, appropriate areas of functioning in the patient contributes to the basic matrix of the analytic relationship. Initially, there may be undistorted expectations of the analytic treatment, and valid conscious and unconscious perceptions of the analyst's ability to be helpful. In addition, there may be the patient's early and expanding capacities for basic trust in the analyst, for developing a secure object relationship with him, and for utilizing nonconflicted ego functions that sustain the analytic work. This includes *preformed nontransferences*—the initial, nondistorted anticipations of the analyst and analytic experience which are the basis for the patient's reasonable expectations of cure. They also entail the patient's general capacities for control, management of his inner state and impulses, modulation of his instinctual drives, ability to maintain perspective on his transference-based reactions and fantasies, and nonpathological superego and ego-ideal functions. They are the nondistorted contributions of the patient to the basic analytic relationship and work, and are the slowly changing, more realistic and appropriate dimensions of his interaction with the analyst.

Matrix nontransference elements draw genetically upon constructive relationships in the patient's childhood, especially with his mothering figure. They involve non-pathological identifications which will be reinforced through identification and introjective identification with an adequately functioning analyst. They may also be influenced to some extent by current realities outside the analytic relationship, and need not be altogether positively-toned, since they will include the patient's realistic expectations of a painful but necessary therapeutic experience, and well-modulated, appropriate positive (erotic) and negative (hostile) feelings. They may therefore contain limited, well-controlled, relatively neutralized libidinal and aggressive elements, and need not be drive-free. These nontransference components constitute a major, but not total, contribution from the patient to the therapeutic alliance.

Reactive Nontransference. These elements comprise those components of the patient's reactions to the analyst and analytic situation that are appropriate to the realistic conditions that prevail at a given moment. They include responses by the patient to outside relationships that influence the therapeutic interaction in a nondistorted manner. They are part of the patient's constructive adaptive efforts to deal with continuing stimuli and trauma, and they show a rapid rate of change.

Reactive nontransference components are a part of the patient's daily reactions to the analyst and are not restricted to positive responses. On the one hand, when the analyst has intervened constructively, they entail appropriate appreciation, nonpathological introjective identifications, and other positive reactions based on a valid perception of his helpfulness. On the other hand, with an analyst who has erred, been unnecessarily hurtful, or who has created a disrupted bipersonal field, negative responses such as doubts regarding the analytic situation and analyst, resentment, a controlled measure of anger, and negatively-toned introjects would have major non-transference elements. In fact, blind acceptance of an analyst's erroneous behavior is actually a distorted and therefore transference-based reaction. Under such conditions, a more questioning and doubtful attitude is far more appropriate and, if such errors are repeated, consideration of termination may well fall into the realm of primarily nontransference responses. The patient has a wide range of possible nontransference reactions to the analyst, a variety of means of expressing them, and a number of basic motives that determine their presence.

The Patient's Accurate Perceptions of and Valid Interactions with the Analyst

If unconscious fantasies and introjects are the core of transference reactions, then intact ego functions, healthy identifications, and veridical unconscious perceptions are at the heart of nontransference responses. Similarly, to the extent that pathological projective and introjective identifications are the essential interactional mechanisms for transference-based interactions, their valid use is the central interactional process for the nonpathological aspects of the analytic interaction. While at times the patient's conscious perceptions of the analyst are basically realistic—much as a conscious fantasy occasionally may correspond quite specifically to an unconscious transference fantasy—the more frequent and crucial nontransference intrapsychic process is that of the patient's undistorted elaborations of his unconscious perceptions. Thus, just as transference reactions are evoked by certain actualities which, in addition to their veridical core, may be primarily or secondarily distorted, nontransference reactions are based on valid unconscious perceptions, and the point at which distortions appear marks the addition of transference elements.

Unconscious perception, as it applies to the analytic interaction, actually includes and extends into a variety of processes in addition to those in the perceptual sphere. It encompasses cognitive understanding, empathic reactions, nonpathogenic introjective identifications, awareness of the analyst's efforts to projectively identify into the patient, nonpathological identifications with the analyst's internal and external objects, and other unconscious processes that lead to or involve nondistorted, valid, and adaptive functioning. These processes are, of course, composed of a variety of specific ego functions, including object relatedness, flexibility in ego boundaries, perception, judgment, and reality testing—among others. They form a conglomerate of nontransference functions that operate on many levels, and can be conceptualized along a number of different lines. They crystallize for each patient into a particular style of expressing his mature, adaptive, appropriate responses to the analyst.

The patient's undistorted, integrative responses to accurate and helpful interventions and managements of the ground rules can lead to acceptance and introjection, and ultimately to cognitive insights and positive incorporative identifications that promote adaptive structural change. They are therefore essential to positive therapeutic outcome. In addition, conscious and especially unconscious perceptions and introjections of the analyst's errors and countertransference difficulties can lead to appropriate nontransference responses on several levels. These include negative introjective identifications with the disturbed analyst, valid curative efforts directed toward this introject and toward the analyst himself, other endeavors to assist the analyst in recognizing and modifying his difficulties, and more direct nontransference responses such as anger, criticism, and disturbances in the interpersonal relationship. Thus, apparent regressions and difficulties in the analytic relationship are not only based on disruptive transference reactions, but may stem from important nontransference responses.

The patient continuously monitors, consciously and unconsciously, the expressions of the analyst's personality and character, style of working, sensitivities and insensitivities, and vulnerabilities and assets as expressed in his silences and interventions. Nontransference reactions pertain both to the analyst's immediate interventions and to his broader attributes and attitudes; these are processed by the analysand in keeping with both transference and nontransference needs and components. Often, the identification of a transference response depends on establishing the limits of the patient's nontransference reactions.

The Identification of Nontransference Elements

Technically, the establishment of the nontransference aspects of the patient's reactions to the analyst's immediate interventions and his more durable character and personality traits relies on the evaluative and validating processes already described. Identification of nontransference expressions in response to a particular intervention or effort at management of the frame depends on a clear-cut assessment of the manifest and latent nature of the patient's communications and a thorough understanding of the specific adaptive context that has evoked them, a study of the analyst's subjective reactions, and a full application of the validating process to the patient's material and the continued subjective reactions of the analyst as it pertains to the initial assessment. Nontransference reactions to the analyst's more durable traits can be detected through an exploration of acute disturbances in the analytic interaction that especially bear on these particular problems. In addition, a most useful clue is the appearance of repetitive patterns of reaction or perception within a given patient without evidence for transference distortions, and similar repetitive responses across the patient population of a particular analyst.

The recognition of appropriate reactions to the analyst's constructive attitudes and continuing work requires no special interventions from the analyst. On the other hand, the patient's realistic responses to the analyst's technical difficulties and countertransferences calls for their *implicit* acknowledgment, the modification of the difficulty within the analyst—rectification—and analytic working through of the effects on the patient. However, since the analysand's responses under these conditions will tend to be an intermixture of transference and nontransference, his appropriate reactions must be separated from those that are inappropriate, and the analytic work must ultimately include an investigation of the ways in which he uses these perceptions to fulfill his own unconscious transference needs. On the other hand, the patient's reactions should not be treated as entirely inappropriate; a balanced approach is essential.

It is also important to establish the genetic resonances for the analysand when the analyst has erred. These are not to be viewed in the sense that the patient brings a distortion to the analytic relationship based on earlier relationships, but rather as indicating that the analyst's traumatizing behavior has actually on some level repeated a pathogenic interaction with an earlier figure. The simultaneous rectification of the disruptive behavior and interpretive work by the analyst goes a long way toward restoring the therapeutic qualities of the bipersonal field, the positive image of the analyst, and the quest for positive inner change for the patient.

In this connection, it is essential that the analyst have the capacity to identify those projective identifications that are based on his own countertransference-related behaviors and which create pathological introjective identifications in the analysand. Modification of the consequences of such identificatory processes within a patient is not feasible without a recognition of the essential elements of truth on which they are based, the correction of these realities, the cessation by the analyst of the expression of the pathological projective identifications, and the analytic understanding of the consequences for the patient. Under such conditions, patients often will make unconscious efforts to maintain sectors of misalliance and areas of shared neurotic gratification and defensiveness, or will attempt to exploit the analyst's vulnerabilities for their own neurotic gain. They will also reproject pathological contents into the analyst who, if unwary, will give way to further pathological reprojections in lieu of sound interpretive efforts.

Benefits derived from the patient's nontransference-based curative efforts, while not the primary purpose of the analytic interaction, can be of considerable help to the analyst; all such gains, however, should be silently accepted without direct acknowledgment. They are best reflected in the resolution of the analyst's countertransference difficulties and in his ability to restore the necessary therapeutic qualities to the bipersonal field and analytic interaction, and to interpret properly to the patient. By fully analyzing the implications of these experiences for the patient, without undue guilt or inappropriate unconscious sanction of a misalliance or other inappropriate behaviors, and through persistent attention to the psychic and external realities that prevail in his interaction with the patient, the analyst can consistently delineate the transference and nontransference components of his patient's communications and intervene appropriately on that basis. Thus, he maintains his own psychic equilibrium, and more importantly, a sound therapeutic alliance with the patient and a properly managed, therapeutic bipersonal field.

This completes my discussion of the patient's relationship with the analyst. It seems evident that such artificial divisions as *transference relationship* or *real relationship* unduly isolate the intermixed sectors of the patient's responses to the analyst, and that the use of the term *transference* to characterize the patient's total relationship to the analyst is essentially inaccurate. It appears best to allude to this relationship as such, and to distinguish as far as possible its transference and nontransference components. It is also important to recognize its intrapsychic and interactional dimensions, and to consider both fully in examining any segment of the analytic interaction. Finally, it is more than evident that it is virtually impossible to validly separate the patient's relationship with the analyst from the analyst's with the patient, although I have done so. I shall now turn to a rather segregated study of the other half of the analytic relationship—that of the analyst to analysand.

Chapter 4

The Analyst's Relationship
to the Patient

Countertransference Reactions

In many ways, the classifications of transference and nontransference developed for the patient's relationship with the analyst can be used to define the analyst's relationship to the patient. Ideally, the differences between the analyst and analysand are largely quantitative—though they may also be, at times, qualitative. They arise primarily from two factors: the achievements of the analyst's own analysis and analytic training, and the differences between his roles and responsibilities and those assigned to the patient—that is, the specific conditions of the analytic relationship and the bipersonal field within which it unfolds.

There are those who prefer to define countertransference as the analyst's pathological reactions to the patient's behaviors and communications, and who endeavor to distinguish these difficulties from the analyst's transferences to the patient, which are seen as pathological elements derived essentially from the analyst's own inner disturbances, that the analyst brings to the relationship. While this distinction may be of some use and will be reflected to some extent in my efforts to delineate matrix and reactive forms of countertransference, both the universality of intermixtures of these two types of pathological expressions in the analyst and current clinical usage suggest that the term *countertransference* be used to refer to all reactions in the analyst based on distorting intrapsychic fantasies and introjects, and therefore essentially inappropriate to the realities of the analytic situation and the patient's therapeutic needs. By and large, the countertransference reactions of the analyst appear directly in his interaction with the patient, although they can be expressed—more often than is usually recognized—in displacements to other patients and outside figures. Countertransference expressions are compromise formations that derive from the inner pathology of the analyst, the status of the bipersonal field, the general and specific adaptive stimuli created by a given patient, and contributions from other realities. Let us now examine their dimensions.

Matrix and Reactive
Countertransference Responses

Matrix Countertransferences. The analyst's countertransference responses may contribute to the basic interactional matrix between the patient and himself in several ways. Despite their distorted and inappropriate qualities, they may be part of or may prompt efforts by the analyst to establish an essentially sound relationship with his patient, although at some point their inappropriate elements will interfere and require modification through self-analysis. Ideally, the analyst ought to resolve all of the unconscious countertransference fantasies, memories, and introjects that influence his basic relationship with the patient; in practice, it is not feasible to do so fully, although it is his responsibility consistently to strive to achieve a maximum degree of mastery. This is especially necessary because the analyst's fundamental mode of relating to and interacting with the patient, and of offering a basic therapeutic hold, is undermined or disturbed by these relatively stable, matrix countertransference factors.

Often, these countertransference-based disturbances relate to anxieties and conflicts regarding the analyst's essential functions as the observer, interpreter, and creator of the bipersonal field within which the analytic process occurs. There are strong maternal and paternal unconscious elements, and in addition to these fundamental problems, the analyst may have a specific countertransference difficulty in establishing the basic analytic relationship with a particular patient. Matrix countertransference difficulties are characteristically chronic in nature and are often derived from the analyst's characterological and more enduring unresolved problems; they tend to be difficult to identify and to resolve (see below).

Reactive Countertransferences. Reactive countertransference responses are generally rather acute, changeable, inappropriate reactions of the analyst to his patient, prompted by immediate adaptive tasks which mobilize distorting intrapsychic fantasies, introjects, and interactional processes. Although they stem, as a rule, largely from the specific interaction with the patient with whom the analyst expresses his countertransference difficulty, they may be evoked by all kinds of stimuli external to that particular analytic relationship.

Reactive countertransferences are most often prompted by the fluctuations in the attributes of a given patient and by the nature of the conscious and unconscious material with which he is dealing from moment to moment. They may stem from more chronic and characterological countertransference difficulties, or may relate to acute disequilibria in the analyst created by the immediate situation within, and in part outside, a given analysis. They constitute the inevitable vulnerabilities of the analyst in his daily analytic work, and ideally should be readily identified, quickly resolved through self-analysis, relatively minor, and not especially repetitive. They tend to be more manageable than matrix countertransference problems, which are more difficult to detect, to trace to the basic unconscious countertransference fantasies involved, and to resolve. Finally, while both types of countertransference responses are ultimately detrimental to the analytic work, as a dimension of the interaction with the analysand, they may nonetheless be utilized to understand his unconscious conflicts, fantasies, and introjects. The stimulus from the patient for a countertransference response will always bear some relationship, major or minor, to the analyst's distorted reaction.

The Sources of
Countertransference Reactions

Genetic Countertransferences.   Classical or genetic countertransferences stem from the analyst's unconscious fantasies, memories, and introjects that are derived from his earlier pathogenic relationships. The analyst responds inappropriately, in terms of an earlier relationship, to the current behaviors and communications from the patient. In one paradigm, a specific patient comes to represent an earlier figure for the analyst. In other situations, the analyst responds to particular associations from the patient in terms of earlier disturbing relationships and experiences, and he may react similarly to outside figures in the analysand's life. The analyst may also inappropriately attempt to use the patient to resolve countertransference difficulties evoked by other patients or by outside figures in his own life. All types of countertransference reactions ultimately have important genetic components.

Countertransference-Based Displacements from Current External Objects. A central factor in the countertransference reaction to a particular patient may derive from a displacement of some conflict or pathological unconscious fantasy that relates primarily to another person toward whom the analyst is relating—an external object. Thus, an intrapsychic or interactional disturbance evoked by another patient, by someone in the analyst's professional world, or by an individual in the sphere of the analyst's social relationships may prompt a countertransference-based response through displacement onto a given analysand. While these displaced reactions characteristically have important genetic roots and always include an unconscious transference fantasy related to the analysand with whom the analyst expresses his difficulty, this category of countertransference reactions underscores the importance of external adaptive contexts and the need for the analyst to self-analyze and resolve the intrapsychic conflicts related to the primary source of his difficulty. Clearly, the resolution of this type of countertransference reaction requires the working through of problems in two current spheres—that related to the patient at hand and that with the person who is the major source of the conflict. Such work, as a rule, will lead the analyst toward genetic roots and interactional transference mechanisms which can then too be self-analytically resolved.

Projective Countertransferences and Projective Identificatory Countertransferences. This extremely important source of countertransference-based interventions is often difficult for the analyst to detect and modify. In the primarily intrapsychic form, the analyst projects onto the patient— attributes to him—some aspect or derivative of his own intrapsychic conflicts and unconscious fantasies, as they reflect the dynamic expression of each of his psychic structures or of his self-representation or introjects. In its interactional form, the analyst, through his counter-transference-based interventions and mismanagements of the frame, inappropriately projectively identifies into the patient selected aspects of his own pathological inner state. The very nature of the analytic relationship and the respective roles of each participant provide the analyst with many opportunities for such projective identifications. Needs of this kind are among the most prominent unconscious motives for becoming a therapist or analyst; placing sick contents into the analysand so as to disown them, evoke proxies, and to work them over externally is an extremely common occurrence. Every intervention that the analyst formulates should be examined for this possibility and his handling of every issue related to the frame should be similarly investigated. These processes, with their underlying pathological motives and genetic components, are undoubtedly the commonest interaction-al source, and form, of countertransference expressions.

Countertransference-Based Identifications, Introjective Identifications, and Projective Counteridentifications. Intrapsychically, there may be in the analyst unconscious needs to inappropriately identify with and support aspects of the patient's pathological inner mental life and behaviors. The analyst may become relatively fixed in these identifications, and thereby experience impairments in the usual, noncountertransference-based process of trial identification with the patient's inner structures and objects, the identificatory aspects of empathy, and other more healthy efforts of this kind. These unconscious identificatory needs often form the basis for sectors of misalliance and for areas of inappropriate mutual identification and living out. They lead to blind spots and to biases that interfere with the analyst's interpretive work and management of the frame.

Interactionally, there are pathological forms of introjective identification that disturb the analytic field and work, including the analyst's comprehension of, and his actual relationship with, the patient. Within the analyst may be inordinate and inappropriate needs to introject and contain pathological and healthy parts of the patient, problems communicated through the analyst's interventions and managements. They lead to countertransference-based efforts to generate disturbances in the patient or to have him serve as the more healthy partner to the analytic dyad. Such exaggerated "introjective hunger" will have disruptive effects on the analytic process.

Another pathological form of introjective identification has been termed *projective counteridentification;* this involves situations in which the analyst's own pathological needs for defense and gratification lead him to incorporate projective identifications from the patient without conscious awareness or control over the processes involved. As a result, he does not metabolize the introjective identification toward interpretive insights, but instead uses the patient's projective identification as an opportunity to express his own countertransference-based needs and reprojects the pathological conglomerate derived from himself and the patient back into the analysand. This creates a rather common disruptive sequence in which there is an unconscious exchange of projective and introjective identifications that are markedly pathological and not processed toward insight and inner structural change for the patient.

While they do contain the potential basis for understanding the analysand, these countertransference-based incorporative identificatory processes tend largely to disturb the analyst's functioning and to place aspects of his pathology into the bipersonal field and patient. Further, by unconsciously accepting aspects of the patient's pathological inner self—for example, his sense of guilt or inappropriate wishes—the analyst becomes involved in a neurotic vicious circle with the analysand that precludes insightful work. Here, too, the analyst's direct involvement in these processes makes detection of their presence, and of the sectors of misalliance that they create, quite difficult.

The Forms of Countertransference Expression

There is a potential for countertransference expression in every intervention by the analyst, in every period in which he is silent, and in every aspect of his management of the framework. In his work with a particular patient, the analyst must continuously scrutinize his inner experiences, indeed, every affect, thought, and fantasy, for a countertransference component. Furthermore, he must do so in his ever-present self-analysis of his outside fantasies and dreams. While this is an onerous and necessary task, it should be feasible for the analyst to quietly monitor his inner experiences and external professional and nonprofessional life for any countertransference-based influences.

The actual expressions or forms taken by derivatives of unconscious countertransference fantasies and introjects parallel those delineated for transference (chapter 3). They may emerge in the form of conscious fantasies toward the particular patient involved, or toward others through displacement; they may be reenacted or lived out in the analytic relationship or with persons other than the particular patient involved; they may appear as direct wishes for extratherapeutic gratification, including instinctualized countertransferences with conscious wishes for sexual and aggressive satisfaction; they may occur as inappropriate beliefs and misconceptions, as other forms of intentions, and even as delusions or hallucinations if the pathology in the analyst is severe; and they may be expressed in symptomatic form. There are also, of course, neurotic, borderline, narcissistic, and psychotic countertransference syndromes, as well as those that may be classified according to basic personality characteristics.

Among the most important expressions of unconscious countertransference fantasies and introjects are those that occur in the analyst's direct interaction with the patient—efforts at reenactment and the expression of pathological interactional processes. These include not only the more familiar forms of technical errors, failures to understand the patient, impairments in empathy, mismanagements of the framework, and incorrect interpretations, but also assume forms of more subtle, indirect, nonverbal and interactional countertransference-based communications and pressures. These more implicit aspects involve unconscious invitations to the patient to participate in the

creation of split-off sectors of the bipersonal field—
bastions—and in the development of sectors of misalliance
that gratify pathological needs and defenses for the
analyst. In the cognitive sphere, repeated failures to
understand and interpret an aspect of the patient's
material may be based on unconscious countertransferences, while interactionally these difficulties may stem
from wishes to harm or seduce, rather than help, the
patient. While countertransference expressions are ultimately based on responses and needs involving earlier objects that determine the analyst's reactions to the analysand, they also reflect current, maladaptive and pathological quests for inappropriate gratification and defense.

The consequences of unconscious countertransference
fantasies and needs may take a form that is relatively well
controlled or one that is blatantly enacted with the
analysand. The analyst may maintain a perspective on his
countertransference based wishes and their manifestations or he may momentarily, or in a more lasting way, lose
sight of the *countertransference illusion*, and accept as valid his
inappropriate reactions to the patient. The factors
involved are comparable to those related to maintaining
perspective and distance from transference-based wishes
and needs—the so-called "transference illusion" (see
chapter 3): they include the use of a variety of ego
functions, the capacity to manage and modulate instinctual drives (the intensity of which is also a factor), superego
and ego-ideal contributions, and the nature and power of
the stimulus emanating from the analysand. Also to be
considered is the assistance of a secure frame which helps
to ensure the boundaries of the analytic relationship, the
implications of all experiences that occur within it, and the
roles and functions of each participant. Any need
experienced by the analyst toward his patient other than

those related to validated interpretations and managements of the framework should be examined for possible loss of perspective and for countertransference-based contributions.

Active and Passive Forms of Countertransference Difficulties. Utilizing an overlapping classification in which the extremes may be more clearly identified, we may think of countertransference problems that stem from below (actively expressed), and those that stem from above (more passively experienced). The former are the active intrapsychic unconscious fantasies, conflicts, and needs that prompt the analyst to respond selectively and inappropriately to the communications from the patient, on the basis of his own distorting inner requirements. These countertransferences, derived from the inner stirrings of the analyst, lead him to react to the basic analytic situation and to selective stimuli from the patient with distorted perceptions, wishes, behaviors, and interactional mechanisms, and also to attempt, unconsciously, to evoke reactions from the patient in keeping with the analyst's own disturbed inner reality and needs.

Countertransferences from above are those inappropriate and distorted responses that emerge from the analyst's attempts to master traumatizing behaviors by the patient and grossly disturbing external life events and relationships. Here, the analyst is less the active provocator and more the passive recipient.

Interactionally, in the first situation it is the analyst who projectively identifies pathological contents into the analysand or invites unneeded pathological projective identifications on the basis of his own active incorporative needs. In the second situation, the analyst tends to be the recipient of the patient's pathological projective identifications or incorporative needs without actively seeking them out, though he nonetheless fails to adequately metabolize them.

The Predominant Functions of a Countertransference Reaction. Because of the nature of the analytic relationship and the bipersonal field, there is relatively little parallel between the functions of transference and countertransference expressions. Transference constitutes pathological distortions and interactions that are appropriate to the role of the analysand, and while they may be disruptive, they always encompass and serve as the ultimate wish for and vehicle of cure. By contrast, countertransference entails pathological distortions and interactions that are essentially inappropriate to the analyst's role, and while they too almost always contain curative threads and wishes, these are largely overshadowed by the pathological elements. Thus, while transference is the inevitable vehicle of cure for the patient, the same does not apply to the analyst's countertransferences: the analytic bipersonal field is not designed for the resolution of his intrapsychic pathology, although it will inevitably afford him some gains in this area.

Countertransference expressions therefore function predominantly as impediments to analytic progress and are disruptive to the analyst's adequate functioning. They generally reflect the intrapsychic resistances of the analyst and contribute to other resistances that are shared with the analysand. Their resolution is not a primary function of the analytic relationship; however, when countertransferences predominate, the cure of the analyst will momentarily (and inappropriately) prevail. Insights into the analyst derived from his countertransference expressions should be the province of his own personal analysis or self-analysis.

Despite these disruptive aspects, countertransference reactions, since they are shaped by and related to the patient's associations and behaviors, can be utilized for understanding the analysand. They may reflect aspects of the latter's pathological unconscious fantasies and introjects, reveal roles and images that he is trying to evoke in the analyst, and echo his use of pathological interactional mechanisms. There may be direct parallels between unconscious elements in the patient and analyst, or the analyst's response may be different and significantly distorted by his own intrapsychic pathology. In this latter instance, however, through self-knowledge, self-analysis of countertransference reactions, and extensive use of the validating process, the analyst can come to know the kernels of a valid understanding of the analysand (and often of embedded positive therapeutic intention) that may be derived from his countertransference reaction— both its underlying unconscious fantasy and its derivative, surface expression.

Lastly, countertransference responses may reflect pathological disturbances in the containing functions of the analyst (see chapter 5). They may modify his basic analytic hold of the analysand and express his refractoriness or overeagerness for containing the patient's pathological contents. Interactionally, then, countertransferences may serve to ward off the patient's projective identifications, or, paradoxically, to inappropriately invite pathological projective identifications and communications from the patient.

The Clinical Determination of a Countertransference Problem. The processes through which the analyst detects the existence of a derivative expression of an unconscious countertransference fantasy and introject are not unlike the means through which he establishes the presence of a transference reaction. However, because of the special conditions deriving from the fact that the analyst is attempting to understand aspects of his own functioning and experiencing, a number of distinctive difficulties arise. There is a general tendency for analysts to search for the sickness and unconscious fantasies and processes that prevail within the analysand, while stressing their own valid functioning and conscious processes. Such inequities in themselves reflect countertransference difficulties, and constant monitoring by the analyst of his own inner experiences and of the communications of the analysand for possible relevance to countertransference difficulties is essential.

In formally identifying a countertransference expression, the analyst must consistently assess the shifting adaptive contexts for the reactions of the analysand and himself. In determining the appropriateness of his feelings, fantasies, cognitive impressions, interpretations, and efforts at management of the frame, he must define the realities of the situation within the patient, himself, and their interaction, as well as their distorted elements. Extensive use must be made of the validating process.

The analyst actually has two major sources for these determinations: the patient and himself. Within the bipersonal field, the analysand serves as a living mirror—both truly reflective and distorting—for the analyst. Consciously, and more usually unconsciously, the patient perceives and detects the analyst's problems, takes them into himself through introjective identification or refuses to contain them, and at times, becomes involved in efforts to cure the analyst through a modification of the pathological introjects and through direct, usually unconscious confrontations and interpretations. Silently—and humbly—the analyst can greatly benefit from these efforts, without specifically acknowledging their presence.

His greatest and more appropriate gratitude can be expressed by demonstrating to the patient their salutory effects through an insightful alteration of his underlying countertransference difficulty, and the rectification of its manifestations in the analytic relationship. In addition, the analyst should ultimately interpret the patient's responses to the countertransference expression, including his pathological introjective identifications.

On a more cognitive level, the analyst may make use of the patient's associations and behaviors to identify his countertransference difficulties by searching for manifest and especially latent communications related to perceptions of his problems. In addition, a search for countertransference expressions should be prompted by the presence of general indicators in the material and reactions from the patient, including the appearance of unexplained resistances, symptoms, regressions, disturbances in the therapeutic alliance, living out, and in general any suggestion of an acute disturbance; nonvalidating responses to a specific intervention are also an important clue. While many of these responses will arise from inner disturbances within the patient, the analyst must overcome his bias against recognizing his own contributions. He should be further prepared to acknowledge valid areas of functioning, perceiving, and communicating in the analysand, and should avail himself—though not overuse—this important resource in handling his countertransference problems.

Within the analyst, any hint of an inner disturbance should alert him to the likelihood of a countertransference difficulty: an unusual attitude toward the patient, an uncharacteristic behavior or stance, an awkward or incorrect intervention, a mismanagement of the framework or unneeded use of a deviation in technique, or any sense that something is amiss. The analyst should come to know his own personal countertransference barometers and must undertake an extensive self-analytic study of any inappropriate intrusions, thoughts, or fantasies during or outside of a session. These contain specific derivatives of his unconscious countertransference fantasies, and are an important route to their resolution.

Other clues lie in the analyst's interaction with the patient, and may be derived from a study of the specific antecedents in the material from the analysand—the precipitants of the acute countertransference response. Often this day residue—the specific adaptive task that has evoked the countertransference difficulty—is significantly related to the unconscious countertransference fantasies that form the underlying basis for the analyst's problems. The study of antecedents for the analyst's errors in techniques, subjective discomfort, or intrusions should be supplemented by an investigation of the patient's subsequent associations. In all, any indication of a countertransference expression in one sphere calls for full use of the validating process with the use of all possible resources.

Technical Implications of Recognized Countertransferences. While a well-controlled countertransference reaction may be limited to the subjective experience of the analyst and resolved before it influences his interaction with the patient to any significant extent, most expressions of unconscious countertransference fantasies that come to the analyst's attention have been translated into errors in intervening or interpreting, mismanagements of the framework, or evidently disturbed basic attitudes toward the analysand. Once these manifestations have been identified and validated, the analyst has the following responsibilities:

1. To modify the underlying basis for the difficulty through a period of self-analysis, carried out separately from the interaction with the patient—although in urgent circumstances this may momentarily preoccupy the analyst during a session.

2. To rectify the effects of the error or mismanagement either by restoring the appropriate framework with the analysand or by subsequently offering the pertinent and correct interpretation when the material from the patient permits.

3. To explore and work through the patient's conscious and unconscious perceptions and introjections of the error, his responses to the analyst's *implicit* acknowledgment of the difficulty, and his reaction to the analyst's resolution of the disturbance.

4. Explicit acknowledgment of the error in technique is in itself a modification in the framework and will usually impair the analyst's basic hold of the analysand; implicit acceptance that includes treating the patient's conscious and unconscious perceptions, and his appropriate direct and indirect responses, as nondistorted and essentially nontransference expressions, supports the patient's inner and outer reality testing and his adaptive capacities. It is therefore sufficient that the analyst's behavior and communications imply the recognition of the error that he has made, reflect his efforts to correct it, and include an understanding of the patient's valid responses. The analytic work must then maintain its focus on the patient's neurotic difficulties and, eventually, where needed, on the distorted components of his reactions to the analyst's problem.

The modification and working through of the effects of countertransference difficulties must take precedence over other adaptive and therapeutic tasks. Any major trauma that occurs in the life of the patient or in the analytic interaction must share the analytic focus with this endeavor.

The Management of the Analyst's Countertransferences

The analyst's task of managing his intrapsychic state, interactional needs, and pathological impulses as they are influenced by his experiences with the patient and secondarily by other relationships is subject to an ever-present, unresolved pressure to achieve counter-transference-based gratifications and defensive misalliances, and to find inappropriate satisfactions in the patient's transference responses and symptoms—which he may unconsciously reinforce. The analyst is confronted on some level with two contradictory wishes: to cure the patient (and himself), and to maintain the patient's illness (as well as his own). In the analyzed analyst, the pursuit of healthy adaptations predominates and self-analysis assists him at those inevitable moments when maladaptive thrusts temporarily take over. Just as for the patient there are appropriate gratifications in his relationship with the analyst and in their pursuit of insight and inner structrual change, so also for the analyst there is a wide range of appropriate satisfactions. These derive from the controlled intimacy of the relationship, the analyst's emphatic experiences, his understanding of the patient, and his correct interpretive and management responses as they afford the patient symptom relief (see below).

Many factors will affect the intermittent countertransference responses that each analyst inevitably develops toward his analysands: the results of his own therapeutic analysis and continuing self-analysis, his life situation, his sensitivities to the qualities of a particular patient, his residual neurotic difficulties, and the nature of his personality, character structure, and psychopathology. At times, these may coalesce into what has been termed a *countertransference neurosis,* although a closer examination of this syndrome as usually described reveals both counter-transference and noncountertransference components. In any meaningful analytic experience, however, it is inevitable that the analyst will have the opportunity to gain some measure of insight and inner structural change; this is a matter of interactional certainty, though it is not the defined goal of the analytic work. It is neither to be preferred or avoided, but it is inherent to a sound analytic experience. It is only when the interface of the bipersonal field shifts predominantly to the sphere of the analyst's pathology, so that his therapeutic needs take precedence, that a disturbed therapeutic situation prevails.

The working through and resolution of the analyst's countertransference responses are essential to the working through and resolution of the patient's transference constellation and the related psychopathology. Thus, the creation of sectors of misalliance based in part on transference- and countertransference-based interactions is on one level a threat to analytic outcome, but on another level becomes an important and, at times, not uncommon vehicle for the cure of the patient. The analyst's countertransference syndrome, however, should be a far less predominant segment of the analytic interaction than that derived from the patient's transference components. The analyst's cure should be essentially a byproduct of the patient's analytic experience, supplemented by his own self-analytic endeavors; however, it is among the catalysts of the central therapeutic work that focuses on the cure of the patient.

The analyst is bound to be traumatized at times in any analytic interaction and will then find it necessary to work through the countertransference components of his reactions. Such disturbances may derive either from his own vulnerabilities or from pressures created by the patient's material or by unconscious wishes to harm or seduce the analyst and disrupt his functioning. If the analyst recognizes the inevitability of inner disturbances and the personal benefit that both he and the patient can ultimately derive from resolving them, he will better tolerate their occurrence and is less likely to respond with countertransference-based revenge, seduction, or withdrawal. Instead, he will maintain continued efforts to understand the patient's unconscious motives for being hurtful, and his own responses to these traumas. It is here that the analyst may make special use of a full understanding of his countertransference reaction to appreciate the factors within the analysand that have evoked it. Experiences of this kind help the analyst to develop an ever-widening awareness of his personal equation.

The analyst may also have special difficulties in appropriately accepting the conscious and unconscious therapeutic efforts of the analysand, and in making full use of their potential. The processing of the patient's projective identifications also requires continuous management, since refractoriness to containing such contents and processes will interfere with his empathic responses and comprehension. There is a fine but crucial distinction between blind introjective identification with the patient and the capacity to accept and experience such interactional efforts with a sense of mastery.

The analyst must be able to tolerate and process intensely pathological and potentially disruptive projective identifications, experiencing them consciously as "signal experiences" and properly metabolizing them. Receptivity to the patient includes acceptance without misalliance or reenactment of the patient's projections and projective identifications, assigned roles, and the images that he builds and attempts to actualize of the analyst. Quite often, the contents placed into the analyst, or the role or the image attributed to him, are in conflict with his own self-representations and self-image, and are discordant with his own inner state and needs. The analyst should be capable of accepting and sampling each of these experiences as a means of understanding the intrapsychic state, conflicts, and interactional needs of the analysand, and he should not prematurely intervene so as to refuse to contain or experience the relevant pathological contents or the evoked roles and images. All such interactional pressures should be sampled within limits, metabolized, cognitively understood, and utilized for therapeutic reprojections through interpretations. Full expression and analysis must take precedence; otherwise, the patient will consciously or unconsciously detect and exploit the analyst's vulnerabilities.

Patients will often associate in areas that are traumatic to a particular analyst, touching on topics and fantasies that resonate with his past and present hypersensitivities; they will also in general move toward the more open revelation of relatively primitive intrapsychic contents, which may have disturbing qualities for the analyst. If he is unable to manage the intrapsychic stirrings so created, he may intervene prematurely or incorrectly, unconsciously directing the patient away from an area that is creating anxiety and conflicts for him. Such efforts will generate interactional resistances, reinforcing their intrapsychic basis within the patient. Maintaining an open analytic field and container for the patient's pathological contents is a trying task that must be consistently monitored for countertransference-based disruptions.

The pressures within the analyst to utilize his relationship with the analysand for his own neurotic needs and defensiveness may be grossly or subtly communicated through interventions and failures to intervene, and mismanagements of the frame. Any failure of validation calls for the investigation of such countertransference-based misappropriations of the relationship with the analysand. It is especially common for the analyst to express these needs by attempting to use the patient as a pathological or inappropriate container for his own pathological projective identifications. Interactionally speaking, the analyst's technical errors, through their manifest and latent content, constitute efforts to place his own pathological contents into the patient and, as a rule, to have the patient therapeutically metabolize or suffer with them. The identification of such countertransference-based interactions is possible only in part through a scrutiny of the contents of the analyst's intervention or failure to intervene; it rests primarily on an understanding of the adaptive context for an incorrect intervention, of the interactional pressures from the patient, and especially of the interactional needs and implict communications embedded in the analyst's erroneous technical measure.

It is important to maintain a balanced view of countertransference responses. While the analyst is primarily searching for less conflicted means of understanding his patient, he must also recognize that his inevitable countertransference experiences can secondarily yield for him information about the analysand—and himself—and that the resolution of the disturbances that they create for the bipersonal field can provide the patient with important analytic experiences and understanding—if well managed and handled with insight. It is in this way that the patient can benefit from the analyst's inevitable failures, as may the analyst himself. Countertransferences may well be the greatest obstacle to psychoanalytic cure—perhaps more so than the patient's transference resistances—and yet they are not without their therapeutic potential. Characteristically, most countertransference-based interventions have embedded in their disruptive matrix positive therapeutic elements that can contribute to an effective analytic experience—if recognized and developed. Their therapeutic use and resolution clearly aids the cure of both participants.

The Noncountertransference Reactions of a Psychoanalyst

The analyst's appropriate and realistic responses to the patient embody his noncountertransference reactions and skills within the analytic situation. These functions center upon his role as a special type of healer and are crystallized in his management of the framework and his verbal interventions—especially his interpretations. They create the conditions and understanding through which the patient can achieve symptom alleviation and modification of his pathological character traits through adaptive insight and inner structural change.

Noncountertransference responses derive from a variety of character traits, personality attributes, intellectual and cognitive abilities, affective responses, and more global sensitivities. In the main, they are reflected in the manner in which the analyst creates and maintains the analytic situation, listens openly and freely to the patient's communications, experiences in signal form the images and roles attributed to him, samples and metabolizes the patient's projective identifications, and processes the material from all these sources toward a valid comprehension of the patient. Deriving additional clues from his own subjective reactions, the analyst offers an appropriate management response or a timely interpretation. Noncountertransference includes the analyst's neutrality— maintaining a position equidistant from the patient's psychic structures, self-representations, and inner and outer world, and intervening without personal bias—and it relies upon his adherence to each of the basic ground rules and boundaries of the analytic relationship. It is, of course, the analyst's relatively unconflicted, noncountertransference functioning that gives a personal stamp to his most effective work with the patient.

Matrix and Reactive Noncountertransferences

Matrix Noncountertransferences. Contributing to the analyst's basic hold and to the matrix relationship are on the one hand his nonconflicted humanity, concern for the patient, and physicianly attitude, and on the other his capacity for restraint, tolerance, acceptance of all communications from the patient, renunciation, and establishing limits. In addition to the security conveyed in his basic stance and in his essential containing capacities, he offers the patient a sense of interactional support that derives from his fundamentally analytic attitudes, not from specific manipulations which actually tend to undermine these qualities. In a properly unfolding analysis, the matrix relationship provides a sense of acceptance, security, trust, and reliability for the patient, who, on that basis, can garner the ego strength needed to risk the exposure of his pathological and primitive inner world and can also accrue positive incorporative identifications with the analyst. This basic hold provides certain cohesive yet flexible qualities to the analytic setting and interaction, contributes to and is expressed through a well-maintained frame, and helps to establish a therapeutically viable bipersonal field within which the patient's analytic experience can constructively unfold. These basic noncountertransference functions also contribute to a sound therapeutic alliance.

Reactive Noncountertransferences. Overlapping with the adaptive or functional capacities that contribute to the matrix noncountertransference are a series of daily, reactive noncountertransference functions that are part of the analyst's immediate relationship with the patient. These reactive noncountertransference responses are central to the maintenance of the framework and are in the service of the analyst's ultimate ability to offer correct and well-timed interpretations. They draw upon a number of conscious and unconscious, cognitive and affective, rational and irrational, projective and identificatory functions that I shall briefly describe, moving from the analyst's receptive noncountertransference functioning, to his processing of the data available to him, to the means through which he imparts his understanding to the patient, and then listens once again.

The Forms of
Noncountertransference Expression

The Analyst's Free-Floating Attention, Role Sensitivity, and Receptive Functioning. In the cognitive sphere, the analyst establishes an openly receptive attitude that has been termed his *free-floating attention.* This entails a basically passive mode of listening that is open to all nuances, ideally without bias, and permits a flow within the analyst of unencumbered associations to the patient's material. On a more interactional level, this receptivity includes the free, though limited acceptance of potential roles and images that the analyst samples without enacting. It also entails the open acceptance and containing of the patient's projective identifications—the contents that the patient wishes to place into the analyst—which are again freely sampled in the absence of an immediate need to reproject (see below).

As the analyst listens and experiences freely, there are, as a rule, accompanying associative and organizing activities; he brings his various cognitive functions—memory, comprehension, organization, synthesis, and the like—to bear upon the material from the patient and makes use of the affects, contents, images, and role tendencies that he is experiencing to begin to comprehend the nature of the analysand's communications and interactional propensities. There is a free alternation between the basically receptive mode and a more active and organizing one, with extensive admixture of rational and irrational thinking and imagining.

Empathic, Identificatory, Projective, and Containing Aspects. The analyst receives and experiences the communications from the patient through a variety of intrapsychic and interactional means. These form a group of primary and secondary process dominated modalities that includes empathic listening, in which consciously and unconsciously, actively and passively, the analyst experiences in some immediate way the affects and contents of the patient's communications. The analyst also makes use of a related, receptive set of identificatory processes that are confined to limited, trial identifications through which he attempts to sample and experience parts of the patient's inner self and the manner in which he treats his objects. These processes are on a continuum with those that are more basically interactional and relate to the analyst's controlled incorporative identifications with the contents and inner states placed into him by the patient, and his kindred capacity to contain the latter's pathological contents, consciously experiencing them and processing or metabolizing them.

Each of these interrelated processes represents a complex mode of receptiveness that reflects noncountertransference functioning so long as the analyst permits himself initially to have these experiences consciously or unconsciously, but then ultimately limits them, consciously identifies their components, and isolates them in order to be consciously aware of what is transpiring. With each receptive mode, the analyst may experience some lessening of the boundaries between himself and the analysand, a merging that must be well modulated, easily reversible, and open to conscious scrutiny. Each of these processes is characterized by primarily passive and sometimes active, conscious and unconscious, modes of listening and introjecting, and are freely intermixed with contributions from the analyst which must be ultimately controlled and recognized. The management of these incorporative and identificatory experiences relies on the essential second stage in which the analyst becomes the observer of his own experiences, in order to maintain mastery over them and to utilize them for the comprehension of the analysand.

The analyst also experiences the communications from the patient as the object of the patient's needs, wishes, and impulses. These involve pressures toward action and inappropriate gratification that generate an intensity to the analyst's empathic and identificatory experiences with the patient that both fosters their appreciation and creates the danger of living out. The analyst is treated in reality in a manner comparable to how the analysand responds both to his inner and outer objects, and these actualities must be openly experienced by the analyst without his active participation toward enactment, and then isolated for scrutiny.

Each of these receptive and identificatory processes is vulnerable to disturbance from countertransference difficulties, and must be continuously examined by the analyst; their yield of information must constantly be validated. They rely on a variety of inner functional capacities, such as the analyst's ability to form a sound object relationship with the patient and yet temporarily blur the boundaries between them, to manage his own inner needs, and to handle disturbances in the analytic relationship as they arise from the pathological unconscious fantasies and wishes of either participant. The potential misapplication of these receptive processes in the service of the analyst's countertransference-based needs is great, and repeated use of the analyst's total subjective awareness and of the patient's communications to verify their valid utilization is indicated.

Along different lines, the analyst's receptivity to the patient's material may be characterized as a turning of both conscious and unconscious aspects of his mind toward the patient. His insights into the analysand may stem from both conscious reasoning and the use of derivatives of unconscious understanding that emerge through peripheral thoughts and fantasies, which are then secondarily processed into direct comprehension. It is important to recognize that the analyst can use his own unconscious processes in the noncountertransference sphere, since there is an erroneous tendency in the literature to equate conscious processes with noncountertransference functioning and unconscious processes with countertransference difficulties. One of the most important rewards for the analyst as it pertains to his functioning with the analysand is that of becoming free to utilize his unconscious sensitivities, through his experiences with the patient and by resolving those intrapsychic conflicts that tend to interfere with their open use.

Noncountertransference Projective Identifications. In his listening and intaking functions, the analyst is not entirely passive. Through his confrontations and interpretations he may mobilize particular unconscious fantasies and introjects in the analysand, and thereby contribute to their emergence and communication. His manner of listening and the ways in which he intervenes will either invite or block the expression of derivatives from the patient. As part of the interactional aspects of these communicative processes, the patient will either enhance or attempt to interfere with the analyst's empathic, identificatory, and introjective functions.

In another sphere and within limits, certain unconscious projective identifications by the analyst into the patient may develop the latter's communicative potential. These projections may place into the patient good parts of the analyst and positive aspects of his functioning. In addition, it may well be that by projectively identifying certain inner states and contents into the patient, so long as these are in very small and controlled doses, the analyst can learn a great deal from the manner in which the patient processes and metabolizes them. However, the danger of countertransference-based use of such projective identifications and their potential for disturbing both the patient and the analytic interaction should caution the analyst to manage these projective processes carefully and to monitor them continually for his own pathological use.

Processing the Data Received from the Patient. The analyst's affectively-toned, conscious, cognitive understanding of the patient is the final common pathway for all of his receptive experiences as he listens and reacts. If he is relatively unencumbered by countertransference difficulties, and is both cognitively adept and interactionally sensitive, these experiences will be verbally formulated on the basis of clues derived from the material from the patient, the interactional experience with him, the analyst's professional training, and his general understanding of human beings, human nature, and himself. The analyst here makes use of a wide range of functional capacities—ego functions and unconscious cognitive tools, as well as his special abilities for synthesis and comprehension.

There are several aspects of the analyst's receptive and integrative functions that merit separate note. First, there is the importance of the analyst's openness toward the patient, balanced with sufficient controls and management. He is prepared to become aware of and experience a variety of budding reactions—for example anger, sexual stimulation, depression, feelings of degradation, pressures to act in a particular way, and evoked fantasies—and yet, through the use of his ego functions, he consistently maintains his perspective on these stirrings and keeps them within certain ill-defined limits. In other terms, these are *signal experiences*—small and controlled doses of what otherwise would develop into more uncontrolled and direct reactions to the patient.

Second, the analyst will not infrequently respond to the

communications from the patient with conscious fantasies that are on some level intimately connected with the intrapsychic state of the analysand. They constitute part of the analyst's immediate, noncognitive processing of the patient's associations and are usually both affectively toned and under the sway of the analyst's primary process functioning. These fantasies, may, of course, either directly refer to the patient or may range into areas that are highly personal or idiosyncratic for the analyst. On the whole, the analyst's cognitive associations to the patient's material are more reality-oriented than his conscious fantasies, and while the latter are especially open to the influence of the analyst's countertransferences, their self-analytic comprehension and resolution offer a unique opportunity for the analyst to get in touch with his own unconscious fantasies vis-à-vis his relationship with the analysand, and thereby with important unconscious fantasies of the patient as well. Here again, validation is essential.

Formally, the analyst's cognitive associations include recollections both of other material from the patient and of previous formulations and the analysand's responses to them, as well as the identification of the adaptive and therapeutic contexts and a variety of other intellectual activities related to the associations at hand. Fantasied responses are usually more dreamlike, often less obviously connected on a manifest level to the associational material from the patient, and always endowed with evident personal elements. When they occur, it behooves the analyst to experience them fully, and then silently to analyze their contents. This is supplemented by continued attention to the patient's associations which, as part of the adaptive context for the analyst's fantasies, will also generally prove relevant. These fantasies are not merely one route to the latent content of the patient's communications, but may also contain special information regarding the analyst's countertransference state. Only after the idiosyncratic components are analyzed will the analyst be able to recognize the latent understanding of the patient contained in his daydream. It is important that these conscious fantasies not be accepted on the manifest level, but be explored for their latent content. Such daydream responses are both inevitable and valuable for the analyst, who must, however, take precautions against being swept away by his fantasizing. Perhaps most crucial in his endeavors to validate these subjective experiences is the search for confirmatory associations from the patient: as a general principle, the analyst should strive to confirm his subjective and interactional experiences through a study of the patient's verbal communications and behaviors; similarly, he should find confirmation of his assessment of the analysand's manifest and latent associations in aspects of his own subjective experiences.

Third, in dealing with the patient's projections and projective identifications, the analyst is faced with special difficulties. He must distinguish what the patient attributes to the analyst that actually stems from within the patient himself from what the patient validly senses as belonging to the analyst. He must determine the validity of the patient's unconscious or conscious perceptions through the validating process. The analyst may defensively and erroneously assess a communication as a projection from the patient in order to deny his own inner contents and state, and the related countertransference-based nature of his interventions or basic stance—factors that interfere with his receptivity and his evaluative capacities.

The task is even more complex where a projective

identification is involved, since this mechanism is interactional; it operates indirectly and largely nonverbally. Here, the analyst becomes aware of certain feelings and fantasies within himself; he examines his own inner state and realities, trying to distinguish those aspects that derive primarily from within himself and those that relate to interactional efforts and pressures from the patient. Since his subjective state is always an intermixture of responses to internal and external stimuli, he also sets about separating each of these components. He finds some assistance in the continued flow and contents of the patient's associations, scanning them for reflections of both the patient's own inner state and projective efforts, and unconscious perceptions and introjections of the analyst.

Processing projective identifications from the analysand involves the capacity to experience the interaction with the patient on the patient's terms, to sort out the sources of the analyst's inner contents, to manage any tendency toward counter-response or rejection of the introject, to obtain confirmation of the analyst's inner feelings and responses from the patient's associations, and then to develop a cognitive formulation that leads to interpretation. Such a process, as I have noted, requires a certain controlled fluidity of ego boundaries, and a capacity to restore separateness when necessary. It is these processes that are most pertinent to the analyst's containing functions, which rely not only on his open availability to the pathological contents from the analysand, but also on his ability properly to metabolize those contents toward an interpretation.

The analyst must be responsive to any shift in the analysand's main sphere of communication; this may develop during one part of a session around verbalized derivatives of unconscious fantasies, and then change to the primary use of interactional mechanisms so that the contents of the analysand's associations become secondary. Determining the most meaningful mode of communication is a difficult task: the analyst must tolerate periods of ambiguity and disruption, create a meaningful dialogue with the analysand, yet accept and understand those moments when contact is broken. He must integrate, separate, imagine, and explicitly formulate. He must generate interpretations and interactional responses, and perhaps most importantly, have sufficient control over the narcissistic investment in his own formulations and interventions, and over other countertransference influences, to permit a realistic assessment of his own and the patient's communications, and to accept valid negative feedback as a guide for reformulation.

The Analyst's Interpretations and Management of the Framework. The analyst's synthetic processes ultimately lead to the crystallization of his comprehension of the communications from the patient into curative interventions. These, as we have seen, fall into two spheres: management of the framework and verbal interventions culminating in interpretations. At times, holding a secure frame for the analysand is the most crucial intervention that the analyst can make. These responses, and his interpretations, have three sources: the internal processing of the analyst, conscious and unconscious processes within the patient, and interactional mechanisms. Ultimately, the analyst's interventions may be best understood as products of the bipersonal analytic field, and as a joint therapeutic effort of the patient and analyst. A large part of the substance of an intervention is placed into the receptive analyst by the analysand (who may also endeavor to deprive the analyst of this important source of understanding). The analyst adds to this the many contributions that have already been discussed.

In managing the frame and in interpreting, the analyst must communicate with clarity, tact, sensitivity, and appropriate timing, and intervene through a modality that reaches the patient in his own idiom through simple and affective language. The basic goal of interpretation must be kept in mind: it is an effort through which the analyst seeks to enable the patient to become aware of pertinent and currently mobilized unconscious fantasies, memories, and introjects; the intrapsychic anxieties and conflicts to which they are related; and the interactional mechanisms and processes that they evoke. To this central core, he will add a comprehension of the current adaptive context for the patient's material, and the pertinent genetic threads.

In concluding, let us note that the analyst should never assume that he is working without a countertransference impediment; he must constantly safeguard his noncountertransference functioning with periods of self-assessment and self-analysis. It is his task to elevate what seems to be a universal capacity for unconscious perception and sensitivity within the analytic relationship to a level of conscious awareness and comprehension. It is here that his task differs significantly from that of the patient, who should eventually take over such functions, but who, for long periods in the psychoanalytic experience, is not in a position to consistently bridge the crucial gap between unconscious perception, fantasy, and interaction on the one hand, and conscious recognition on the other. The patient's essential contribution to the analytic process is his capacity to communicate verbally and interactionally the derivatives of his unconscious fantasies, perceptions, structures, and processes. The analyst's essential contribution must ultimately come from his capacity to maintain a sector of noncountertransference functioning that is used to develop a meaningful relationship within which he imparts conscious cognitive insights and constructive interactional responses to the analysand.

Finally, we may note the analyst's gratifications from his work. These may, of course, relate to the satisfaction of inappropriate and pathological unconscious fantasies, and of defensive and narcissistic needs, that will in turn serve to reinforce the expressions of his countertransference difficulties in his work with his patient unless they are identified and resolved from within. On the other hand, the appropriate satisfactions include his special opportunity to help his patients to resolve their emotional suffering, derived from his appropriate empathic and comprehending functions, and the small or large incidental gains and growth that he derives from his analytic work with each analysand. There are not only a variety of controlled and modulated satisfactions available to him in his daily work with his patients, but also special gratifications to be gained in experiencing successful terminations with his patients, that include the nuances involved in the necessary ending of a meaningful but limited and finite relationship.

Concluding this chapter on such a note reminds us that it has become quite evident that the analytic relationship and all that transpires within it has consistent and crucial interactional components. It is to these that I will now turn.

Chapter 5

Interactional Processes

The psychoanalytic situation is a bipolar, asymmetrical interactional field. Up to this point, I have been focusing on its structure and on its two main polarities. Here, I shall deal with the interactional processes that occur within its sphere. This will include a consideration of the therapeutic alliance and therapeutic misalliances, a study of the basic interactional mechanisms in the analytic relationship, and a conception of the interactional components of certain fundamental processes that have heretofore been characterized primarily in terms of the intrapsychic experience of the patient or analyst—for example, resistances, symptoms, transference, and countertransference.

The Therapeutic Alliance

Historically, transference was viewed by classicial analysts as an essentially intrapsychic phenomenon, and its interactional components largely relegated to the periphery. Similarly, countertransference was seen basically as an intrapsychic occurrence; since it was considered primarily as a response to the analysand, some interactional considerations of a secondary nature were generally included. On the other hand, the realities of the psychoanalytic agreement, arrangements, and ground rules were largely viewed as an interactional pact between the analyst and his patient; the emphasis, however, was on their rational components for both participants. Transference, then, has been considered as irrational and intrapsychic, and the therapeutic alliance as rational and, within some limits, interactional. Basic interactional processes were, however, essentially disregarded in preference for those that are intrapsychic.

The Kleinians, with a virtually exclusive intrapsychic view of both transference and interaction, and with an overriding focus on the patient, tended to ignore the contributions of many aspects of reality and rationality to the therapeutic alliance, and more broadly, to the analytic interaction. At times, too, their study of interactional mechanisms set aside important intrapsychic contributions to these processes, especially those deriving from the analyst. They thereby created a sensitive picture of certain unconscious factors in the analytic interaction, though they removed it from the real world both within and outside the analytic setting, and from important intrapsychic influences.

As a classical psychoanalyst, I became interested in the interactional components of the analytic relationship through a series of explorations of the therapeutic alliance and its disturbances. I soon began to realize that these components were not restricted to the alliance sector, and that they play a profound role in every aspect of the analytic experience. Thus, the therapeutic alliance does not embrace the whole interactional dimension of the analytic relationship, but is in essence a means of isolating a number of crucial factors in this relationship that have a significant bearing on the continuity and effectiveness of the analytic treatment. This alliance is by no means simply based on the realities of the analytic relationship as a rational compact between the healthy parts of the patient and analyst, but contains unconscious and irrational elements. It is therefore not the counterpart or opposite of transference, but is essentially on a different level of conceptualization.

The therapeutic alliance may briefly be defined as the conscious and unconscious agreement of the patient and analyst to join forces in effecting symptom alleviation and characterological modification for the analysand through the achievement of adaptive insights and inner structural change. It is, therefore, basically founded on the patient's wish to constructively modify his emotional difficulties and on the analyst's capacity to create a situation within which this can be accomplished and, specifically, to contribute to this achievement of the patient through his verbal and nonverbal interventions.

While the term *therapeutic alliance* alludes to the whole of this particular sector of the analytic relationship, the term *working alliance* refers to that segment of the analytic relatedness that is essentially based on the patient's rational, nonneurotic wish to get well; on the analyst's rational, nonneurotic offer of assistance and capacity to cooperate with the patient in these efforts; and on their mutual, basically rational efforts to effect a cure. It is based on mutual respect and trust, and the respective capacities in the participants for relatively mature object relatedness and effective analytic work.

Sources of the Alliance

The therapeutic alliance is created through the patient's motivations for cure and the analyst's professional commitment and abilities, and crystallizes around the implicit and explicit analytic pact as it is developed and explicated in the course of the analytic experience. Its evolution is based on the conscious and unconscious motives and needs of both participants, and is continuously influenced by the analytic interaction and by the intrapsychic fluctuations and variations in the ego capacities of each. While in large measure the alliance relies on a variety of stable ego functions, clinically it is possible to establish a relatively secure therapeutic alliance with patients who show impairments in a number of these functions; by contrast, a quite insecure alliance may prevail with a seemingly rational and mature patient. Thus, these fundamental abilities do not contribute to the alliance in a straightforward manner, but in a complex interaction with unconscious factors, including those related to intrapsychic conflicts and instinctual needs, and to interactional processes.

The basic contributions of the patient to the therapeutic alliance lie in his conscious and unconscious motivation and fantasies for seeking treatment, and his rational ideas and fantasies about how the analysis and analytic relationship will unfold. His more realistic expectations, as well as those that are irrational and based on pathogenic unconscious fantasies and unresolved intrapsychic conflicts, are relevant. Both transference-based and more appropriate nontransference expectations and fantasies contribute to the initiation and continuing development of the alliance sector. While the transference elements may at times disturb the alliance and will always ultimately require analytic resolution, they may in part, for long periods of time, contribute positively to the alliance.

The continuation of a secure alliance depends on the maintenance of relatively mature functioning within each participant, and its impairments in this respect stem primarily from disturbances in the patient's basic ego functions and object relatedness, and from similar difficulties within the analyst that interfere with his essential analytic functioning. It is important, however, to recognize the influences of more dynamic factors, many of them related to the effects of the unconscious fantasies, introjects, and intrapsychic conflicts of each participant— transferences and countertransferences. As prompted by experiences within and external to the analysis, the intrapsychic fantasies that are stirred up within the analysand will have an effect on the alliance, as will his capacity to maintain perspective. In addition, unconscious and conflict-related factors influence the ego functioning and object ties necessary for a secure alliance. Their analytic resolution contributes significantly to the mainte- nance of the alliance far more than unneeded deviations in basic analytic technique, undertaken with the misguided rationalization that they are designed to foster the maturation of the patient's effective ego functions and reinforce the alliance. As a rule, these latter measures actually tend to undermine the patient's mature function- ing, while interpretive work with the unconscious transference fantasies that are disturbing the alliance sector will have salutory effects (see below).

The analysand's motivations for analysis and for developing an alliance with the analyst range from the rational wish to find symptom relief through insight, to irrational and magical expectations that include the hope for immediate cure. The patient may enter analysis with a number of inappropriate motives that can be readily modified analytically, yielding positive contributions to the alliance. In addition, there may be a variety of deviant motives that are more difficult to resolve—expectations of actually maintaining or reinforcing the neurosis, or of exploiting the analyst in various inappropriate ways. These motives tend, of course, to contribute to early disturbances in the therapeutic alliance; they must be detected in the opening phase of the analysis and analytically resolved in order to permit the development of a sound therapeutic alliance. Crucial in such work, as is true for any interactional component of the analytic relationship, is the analyst's ability not to join the patient in living out or gratifying his inappropriate wishes—here, in creating a sector of misalliance. Actual nonparticipation is fundamental to the analytic work with the patient, and to creating the conditions under which he will communicate the relevant derivatives of his unconscious wishes in a form that lends itself to valid analytic interventions.

The motivational core of the analyst's contribution to the therapeutic alliance lies in his desire to offer a rational analytic cure. However, each specific patient and the start of each new analytic experience will stir up within him unconscious fantasies and needs that reflect irrational fantasies of cure and noncurative wishes. He must be prepared to detect these more pathogenic stirrings, explore them, control any expression of them within the analytic interaction, and resolve their underlying basis in order to permit the creation of a sound therapeutic alliance and to control his own tendencies toward disturbed alliances and misalliances. Thus, in addition to the relatively autonomous ego functions necessary for the formation of the alliance, mastery of his countertransference tendencies makes an important contribution.

Interactionally, a disturbance within one participant in the analytic situation that is related to any component of the therapeutic alliance will be consciously or unconsciously detected by the other participant, making possible the kind of circular development that leads to a misalliance or other varieties of interactional pathology. Each member of the dyad has impulses toward the development of impairments in the alliance sector and, simultaneously, toward maintaining a sound alliance and resolving the inevitable impairments that arise.

Because the alliance forms an important backdrop for constructive analytic work (though this may occur even in the face of a disrupted therapeutic alliance), and because it is pertinent to the continuation of the analysis, the analyst should consistently monitor this dimension and be prepared to work interpretively on the conscious and unconscious factors within himself and the patient that contribute to disturbances. Among the most important sources of these disruptions are the patient's anxieties and dread of his inner mental contents and the stirrings created by his relationship with the analyst—and therefore, fear of his pathological unconscious fantasies and introjects, especially those that pertain to the analyst. The mobilization of especially painful and traumatic memories, and the consequent repercussions within the patient, may also prove disruptive, as may the experience of regressive symptomatology or relatively uncontrolled living out. The alliance may be temporarily disturbed when the bipersonal field is modified or, paradoxically, when it has been secured; it may be threatened by needs within the analysand for defense and resistance, and for inappropriate gratification. The patient's conscious or unconscious perception of the analyst's countertransference difficulties may also lead to difficulties in the therapeutic alliance. As a rule, as long as the analyst maintains the security of the framework and a basic interpretive stance, the unconscious sources of acute disturbances in the therapeutic alliance will be available from the analysand in derivative form, and therefore analyzable and resolvable. More lasting disturbances in the alliance and premature terminations tend to occur largely when the analyst's countertransference difficulties have contributed significantly to the problems with the alliance and have not been brought under control, and when he unnecessarily modifies the frame.

The ego capacities required for the therapeutic alliance are by no means uniform functions; they are variable within a given patient and fluctuate over time. A secure alliance may be found in patients with severe psychopathology, including paranoid trends, though under such circumstances it is often especially vulnerable to disturbances based on intrapsychic and interactional conflicts and anxieties that disrupt the relatively autonomous capacities of the analysand. In general, the more mature and stable these capacities and functions are in the patient, the more he will be able to effect a strong therapeutic alliance and the more consistent this alliance will be. However, ego dysfunctions are influenced in important ways by intrapsychic conflicts and pathogenic unconscious fantasies and introjects, allowing room for basic analytic work in the face of these dysfunctions.

Genetically, growth promoting and satisfying experiences with the mothering figure—drawn, however, from each stage of development—contribute positively to the alliance, as will such experiences with secondary family and caring figures. Disturbances in maternal care contribute to dysfunctions in the abilities needed for a secure alliance, although such dysfunctions are not solely the product of pathological interactions, since later contributions derived from the patient's own disruptive intrapsychic fantasies and needs are important. There is no basis for a therapeutic nihilism that suggests that without the capacities for basic trust, a variety of fundamental ego functions, and maturity of object relatedness a viable therapeutic alliance and analytic experience are impossible. This reflects a tendency to overlook the role played by fundamental psychoanalytic work in securing the alliance by providing the patient with insight and new adaptive capacities that help to modify his ego dysfunctions, and by implicitly offering the patient opportunities for constructive, broadly ego-strengthening identifications with the analyst that help to stabilize these functions.

In this context, it is to be stressed that in developing a viable therapeutic alliance, there is no substitute for a sound and basic analytic stance, the maintenance of a secure framework, and proper analytic work. As we have seen, when the analyst maintains a sound frame, the patient has an opportunity to incorporate both the communicated ego strengths of the analyst and the solidity of the framework that surrounds the analytic field. He gains a general, increased capacity to tolerate frustration, to maintain boundaries, and to function adequately in the face of anxiety and stress. A stable frame also affords the patient a proper therapeutic field within which to reveal himself and regress, and to utilize and develop cognitive insights and positive introjective identifications offered through the analyst's interpretations.

Among the contributions which the analyst makes to the therapeutic alliance through his basic attitudes and interventions, his interpretations are probably the most important. Ill-advised manipulations such as direct efforts to reassure the patient, advise him, and carry out functions that should be his responsibility—noninterpretive measures that have been advocated supposedly to foster the therapeutic alliance—actually create impairments in the alliance sector by implying a conviction that the patient does not have the capacity to manage his own internal and external affairs, and by invading the patient's essential autonomies. Such manipulations also tend to run counter to the therapeutic alliance by reflecting the analyst's unconscious countertransference-based needs to control the patient, to bypass insightful analytic work and more broadly, to direct the therapeutic field away from basic analytic endeavors. They convey a sense of anxiety and confusion in the analyst which further disrupts any sense of a positive and effective alliance.

Maintaining a basically "neutral" and interpretive position depends on the analyst's capacity to deal with the patient's anxieties and fantasies, to maintain his basic ego functions in the face of threat, and to manage his own countertransference tendencies. Analysts vary in the extent to which they are capable of maintaining relatively conflict-free functioning, especially in the face of acute regressions within the patient. Each analyst has his own characteristic strengths and weaknesses, and here too it is important that he know his personal equation. He can then recognize specific clinical situations in which the alliance is detrimentally influenced by his own problems, and he is in a position to rectify the situation and restore the alliance sector. In all, maintenance of a sound therapeutic alliance depends on the relatively healthy and able aspects of the personality and functioning of both participants, and on the meaningful resolution of the neurotic or more severe disturbances of either participant that encroach upon the alliance sector.

The Analytic Pact

As the basic component of the therapeutic alliance, the analytic pact between the patient and analysand is implicitly and explicitly established through the analyst's delineation of the ground rules and boundaries, and through the patient's responses to the framework. While this includes the patient's capacity for rational cooperation within a secure relationship with the analyst and centers upon the fundamental rule of free association, it also involves an implicit agreement that the patient not only strive to work with the analyst and to understand himself, but also that he produce analyzable derivatives—verbal or behavioral—of his unconscious fantasies, introjects, and conflicts. The analyst, in searching for impairments in the therapeutic alliance, must therefore look beyond the patient's surface cooperation with facets of the analytic pact to more latent and unconsciously determined aspects, such as the analysand's ability to free associate and interact in a manner that presents for analytic work the derivatives of his pathological, inner mental life. The analytic pact, as is true more broadly for the therapeutic alliance, has both conscious and unconscious elements.

Clinically, the analyst who is sensitive to workable derivatives of the patient's unconscious fantasies and introjects will find that the patient unconsciously controls the extent to which he communicates such expressions; often, considerable analytic work is necessary to modify the defenses or misalliances, and the unconscious sources of gratification that generate interferences with their production. The analyst, then, must work not only with verbalized and interactional derivatives from the patient, but also with the analysand's capacity to unconsciously communicate in an analyzable manner. From time to time in every analysis, and quite often with certain analysands, there will be periods when the patient will not associate meaningfully to the analyst on a verbal level, or create an interaction that is open to analytic interpretation.

At other times, the patient may choose to communicate primarily through his behaviors rather than through his verbal associations (see below). The analyst must be sensitive to these less evident impairments in the therapeutic alliance, since his basic analytic work relies on potentially interpretable derivatives from the patient; he must also work within the sphere of the patient's most meaningful communications for the moment, whether in the realm of interaction or verbalization. The unconscious motives for such periods of noncommunication must be detected through a proper understanding of the latent content of the patient's associations and interaction, which include motives that are both intrapsychic (defensive and inappropriately gratifying) and interactional (hostile, seductive, or withdrawal). The unconscious components of the patient's contribution to the therapeutic alliance may be crucial; often a patient may appear to be cooperative on the surface, but is unconsciously disrupting the alliance or attempting to create a sector of misalliance with the analyst. Nonparticipation, detection, and analytic resolution are the essential means of modifying such trends.

Inherent in the analyst's contribution to the analytic pact is his promise to cure the patient and therefore to be tolerant, neutral, controlled, and capable of interpreting where indicated. It is here that interaction again plays an important role. The patient's capacity to develop and maintain a sound therapeutic alliance with the analyst depends not only on factors within himself, but on his conscious and unconscious perceptions of the actualities of the analyst's behavior and competence, and management of the analytic pact itself. The analyst's ability to adhere to the established ground rules, to behave in an effective and concerned manner, and to be sensitive to the patient's anxieties and conflicts, is vital: any countertransference impairment in these attributes will tend to interfere with the alliance.

For the analyst, too, in addition to his announced directives regarding the analytic agreement and his implict creation of additional ground rules and boundaries, much depends on his subsequent management of this pact. Pathological unconscious needs may prompt him to maintain the belief that he is adhering to the pact on the surface, while on a less apparent level he is actually undermining its elements. Self-scrutiny and self-analysis, monitoring and validating, are once again the basic tools through which the analyst safeguards his contributions to the analytic pact and assures the analysand of a consistent attitude, both consciously and unconsciously.

Impairments in the Therapeutic Alliance

The maintenance of the therapeutic alliance, as we have seen, entails the renunciation of wishes for inappropriate gratification and defense by both patient and analyst, and draws upon a variety of capacities to steadfastly pursue analytic goals and dreaded, pathological unconscious fantasies, introjects, and interactions. In the main, there are two types of disruptions in the alliance: essentially unilateral disturbances derived from significant problems in one of the participants, and those that take the form of conscious or unconscious collusion—sectors of therapeutic misalliance. Disturbances in the alliance may also be classified as acute with relatively sudden ruptures in the working relationship, or as insidious and chronic with

generally more subtle though sometimes gross disturbances in this relationship that prevail over longer periods of
time. These impairments may be manifested in a variety of
ways: difficulties in carrying out responsibilities in the
analytic situation; problems in adhering to some aspect of
the ground rules and boundaries of the analytic pact;
conscious reluctance to maintain an analytic atmosphere
and the search for insight and inner change; acute and
sometimes massive resistances against the analytic work;
stalemates; the failure by the analysand to provide
analyzable derivatives and by the analyst to offer timely
interpretations and manage the frame; and sudden
premature terminations.

Unilateral Disturbances Derived Primarily from the Patient.
While every disruption in the therapeutic alliance unfolds
within the framework of the analytic interaction, there
are—more rarely than one might suspect from the
literature—situations where the patient shows a marked
inability to mobilize the ego functions, object relatedness,
and general capacities necessary to maintain a working
relationship with the analyst geared toward valid analytic
goals. The analyst must be wary of the danger of using
such an assessment as a rationalization or defensive cover
for his own unrecognized contributions to a disturbed
therapeutic alliance, or as a way of bypassing the
contribution of more dynamic factors in the analysand. He
must investigate such situations with extraordinary care
and extensive use of the validating process.

There are, however, instances in which the patient's
psychopathology, intrapsychic conflicts, and basic character structure are such that he is unable to generate a secure
sense of trust even with the most effective and concerned
analyst, and is unable to develop the basic motivation

necessary for analytic treatment—in essence, he cannot establish and maintain an alliance. These patients will often enter analysis in an extremely guarded and tentative way, sometimes under pressure from others and, as a rule, with considerable denial of their own inner suffering. Characteristically, as soon as the first significant area of inner disturbance is touched upon, either within or outside the transference aspects of the relationship, they will disrupt the alliance, develop massive resistances, and often take flight from the treatment. Such patients project or projectively identify into the analyst many disturbed parts of themselves, and in addition, frequently anticipate severe traumatization by the analyst in a manner not unlike the very damaging childhood relationships that characterize their early life experiences. They tend to lack the capacity to discriminate between the analyst and these earlier figures, show a general inability to tolerate anxiety, have difficulty distinguishing their inner fantasies from actual outer reality, and have problems separating their projections from the actualities of their relationship with the analyst. They tend to feel endangered by their early memories, inner fantasy life and introjects, and often disrupt the alliance with massive resistances when these inner contents are mobilized, even if this is carried out with extreme caution and tact by the analyst. Quite often a traumatic experience within or outside analysis will mobilize intense unconscious transference fantasies with extremely primitive and disturbing contents which prompt massive efforts at denial and flight, and therefore lead to an acute disruption in the therapeutic alliance. Along different lines, these patients resort to living out in order to secure outside inappropriate gratifications, intensely rationalizing and justifying the presence of realities that are largely determined by their unconscious needs. Buttressed by these outside situations, they lose interest in the analysis, forego the alliance, and often terminate prematurely rather than face the anxieties engendered by a therapeutic regression and a termination experience. Thus, ego impairments are reinforced by upsurges of conflicted contents and disturbing misconceptions of the analytic interaction, precipitated by specific external and internal stimuli.

Technically, with these patients and during such interludes, the analyst attempts first of all to anticipate any potential source of disruption in the therapeutic alliance and focuses his analytic efforts along such lines, using the utmost sensitivity and tact. Interpretation of the unconscious fantasies related to the pertinent anxieties and resistances is most helpful, as is the steady maintenance of a secure frame. With many of these patients, however, the relationship is so guarded and tenuous that the analyst's most sensitive efforts may go unheeded or be experienced by the patient as a dangerous intrusion or seduction against which he must protect himself. As long as the analyst maintains a sympathetic and *implicitly* supportive, nondeviant therapeutic focus on this area of disturbance, he can feel assured that he has made every possible effort to create a proper analytic situation and to preclude the sudden termination of the treatment. It is, however, one of the limitations of analysis that despite the analyst's best efforts there are patients who never truly become engaged in the analytic work; such patients may be suddenly lost to analysis, most often in the opening phase. Yet their existence should not be a self-deceiving rationalization for the analyst's failure to comprehend other sources of disruptions in the therapeutic alliance, especially those that are based in part on his own contributions.

Unilateral Disturbances Derived Primarily from the Analyst. The analyst, too, may unilaterally create disturbances in the therapeutic alliance. These may be based on any type of countertransference problem and reflect his general difficulties in effecting an alliance, or they may involve a specific problem with a given patient. With an unanalyzed therapist, one can repeatedly observe significant disturbances in his interaction with the patient that take the form of unneeded deviations in technique, incorrect and missed interventions, and general human insensitivities— all of which seriously impair the alliance sector. The patient who is subjected to these disruptive influences from the therapist or analyst may respond (1) by exploiting their presence and forming a misalliance, (2) by intensifying his own resistances even to the point of terminating, or (3) by unconsciously attempting to cure the analyst and rectify the difficulty.

Bilateral Impairments: Therapeutic Misalliances. Probably the single most common general disturbance in the therapeutic alliance is one in which to some extent both patient and analyst contribute to and participate in the disruption, thereby creating a sector of therapeutic misalliance. These comprise all those joint conscious and unconscious efforts to interact on some level in a manner that is geared not toward insight and adaptive structural change, but toward some other type of nontherapeutic gratification or defensiveness, or other means of symptom alleviation, however temporary. There are deep and inherent needs for misalliance in both the patient and analyst, and temporary sectors of this kind are inevitable in the course of any analysis. Characteristically, they are a means through which each participant repeats aspects of a past pathogenic relationship, confirms his pathological inner reality, and gratifies his neurotic unconscious fantasies, including their instinctual and defensive elements.

Misalliances are to be detected through the analyst's subjective awareness and by a scrutiny of the manifest and latent content of the patient's associations for relevant communications. They are to be considered in the presence of any disturbance in the analytic work or any discomfort within the analyst. Resolution is based on the unconscious curative efforts of both the patient and analyst, and ultimately relies on the latter's endeavors to rectify and interpret; this constitutes one of the most significant curative experiences in treatment.

A misalliance may be viewed as a form of *interactional neurosis*—or other pathological syndrome—of the patient and analyst; it is an amalgam of their pathological needs and defenses, and takes shape according to the compromise formation that evolves from vectors related to each element in the analytic bipersonal field. It is a shared aspect of pathology with both intrapsychic and interactional components, and may take the form of a disorder in communication in which a bastion of the bipersonal field is created so that a sector is split off, denied or repressed by both participants. It may also take shape as the shared and inappropriate gratification of unconscious fantasies through living out, or may have the characteristics of a reenactment with strong, superego-based, pathological sanctions.

A misalliance, then, may be based on any type of dynamic constellation in which the patient and analyst unconsciously live out a compromise derived from the pathological intrapsychic and interactional needs of each. As an actual form of collusion, its resolution takes precedence over other analytic tasks, and is based on interpretations related to the derivative expressions of the patient's unconscious perceptions of the misalliance and the pathological unconscious fantasies—especially those related to the analyst—that it gratifies. This interpretive work is founded, however, on a rectification of the analyst's participation in the sector of misalliance, since verbal interpretive work will have little effect in the face of expressions from the analyst of a continued need for the sector of misalliance. The analyst should also make use implicitly of the patient's own curative efforts, modifying his participation and interpreting, without denial of his own contributions, the analysand's need for the collusion.

A sector of misalliance constitutes a basic form of pathology of the bipersonal field. As such, it undermines the therapeutic qualities of that field and thereby disrupts insightful analytic work and positive introjective identifications. As a participant in a misalliance, the analyst projects and projectively identifies a variety of negative images that the patient will unconsciously perceive and incorporate. Misalliances tend also to shift the communicative interface of the bipersonal field toward the pathology of the analyst and to interfere with free communication within the field—intrapsychically and interactionally. The resolution of a sector of misalliance therefore restores therapeutic properties to the bipersonal field—another reason that these constitute a prime therapeutic context.

The concept of the therapeutic alliance as understood by classical analysts, while interactional, tends to deal with more superficial aspects and to restrict itself to the efforts of each participant to maintain the motivation for and work directed toward the cure of the patient. Such thinking does not take into account the more continuous interaction between the patient and analyst, nor does it consider the many interactional mechanisms of the total interactional—bipersonal—field. It is to this broader area that I will now turn.

The Basic Interactional Components of the Analytic Relationship

It is in keeping with the history of the psychoanalytic study of the analytic relationship that my last subject of consideration should be the bipersonal field, even though it is probably the most basic dimension of the psychoanalytic situation. As I have noted before, an all-inclusive definition of the bipersonal field will take into consideration the intrapsychic state of each participant, as well as the unconscious interactional processes that characterize their basic relationship. I shall confine myself here to briefly identifying the fundamental aspects of the interactional dimension within the framework of the bipersonal field, and shall offer some brief comments on their many technical implications.

If we conceive of the analytic relationship as unfolding within a bipersonal field defined by the physical arrangements of the analyst's office and the ground rules, and by the agreed-upon boundaries, roles, and rules that characterize this relationship, we may then consider the interactional properties of the field. In doing so, it will also be necessary to characterize its main communicative properties. It should be recognized that these mechanisms may be used by either patient or analyst, that they may be adaptive or maladaptive, pathological or non-pathological, and that in general the more pathological forms should characterize the interactional thrusts of the analysand. The major interactional components are identification and projection, and projective and introjective identification.

Identification and Projection. These processes are basically intrapsychic, although they rely on interaction, and on unconscious perception and fantasy. In brief, identification alludes to the modification of one's self-representations, inner structures, conscious and unconscious fantasies, introjects, and identity or total self in keeping with the perception of another person—"object'—while projection refers to attributing these elements as they exist within one's self to another person.

Projective Identification and Introjective Identification. These are the two most basic interactional processes within the analytic field. Projective identification—that is, interactional projection—refers to interactional efforts to put into another person—the object—one's own inner contents, fantasies, introjects, structures, aspects of the self, self-representations, affects, and other qualities. It is an interactional effort that may be undertaken through indirect communication and is often implicit in what the patient is doing rather than in the manifest content of what he is saying. This process may be utilized in the presence of relatively fluid self-object boundaries, or in a setting of secure self-object differentiation; it has both primitive and more structured forms. It may be based on pathological needs and motives or nonpathological ones, especially those with curative intentions. Its use tends to deplete the subject and to fill the object, and the latter's responses are determined by the nature of the projective identification, his own containing capacities, and his metabolism or processing of the projective identification.

Technically, the analyst relies heavily on his subjective experiences with the patient in identifying the latter's projective identifications, seeking confirmation in the verbal component of the analysand's associations, and consistently endeavoring to discriminate between those aspects of his subjective experience that derive primarily from his own inner strivings and stirrings, and those that are specifically related to the contents being projected into him. The goal is to become conscious of the implications of the projective identification and ultimately to interpret them to the analysand; extensive application of the validating process is essential. As a rule, the analytic resolution of pathological projective identifications takes precedence over the exploration of the patient's verbal associations since they relate to the actualities of the analytic interaction. The pathological projective indentifi-cations may create unconscious sectors of misalliance, disrupt the therapeutic qualities of the bipersonal field, impair its communicative flow, and will tend to be more important for the moment in the patient's adaptive efforts than his intrapsychic conflicts and anxieties.

It is in the processing of the patient's projective identifications that the analyst most clearly expresses his containing functions and capacity to accept into himself the patient's pathological contents, and to metabolize them properly toward an interpretation. Disturbances in this containing function take the following forms: refractoriness, a need to invite pathological contents from the analysand (beyond those that he would ordinarily place into the analyst), and impairments in metabolizing them, so that they are not consciously understood and interpret-ed by the analyst. These disturbances are communicated through the manner in which the analyst listens, misintervenes, or has difficulty in managing the frame-work. In a variety of ways, he unconsciously conveys the positive and disturbed qualities of this function to the analysand.

Another difficult task confronts the analyst as he scrutinizes his interventions to the patient for projective identifications of his own. Every error in intervening and mismanagement of the frame includes some elements of an interactional effort by the analyst to place into the patient, as a pathological and inappropriate container, aspects of his own inner pathology; since such interventions are not in the service of the patient's needs, they reflect the countertransferences of the analyst and interactional efforts to have the patient contain them. A comprehension of these interactional processes includes an understanding of the adaptive context that has evoked the analyst's error, the manifest and latent content of the incorrect intervention, and especially its communicative functions. In assessing such projective identifications, the analyst relies on his subsequent subjective reactions and on the manifest and latent content of his patient's associations. The latter communications reflect the patient's unconscious perception and introjective identification of the analyst's pathology, and include valid perceptions as well as distorted secondary reactions. At times, the patient will be refractory to containing such contents and will protest directly or indirectly, although more characteristically he will introject, serve as a container, and unconsciously attempt both to exploit the analyst's difficulty and to cure him of it.

In investigating such interactional processes, it is important to look for indirect modes of communication, to apply the analyst's self-knowledge, and to use the validating process extensively. Technically, of course, the examination of a planned interpretation for possible projective identificatory elements enables the analyst better to control such expressions of his countertransferences. After intervening, the analyst should always scrutinize the patient's associations and his own subjective reactions for indications of pathological projective and introjective identifications; once discovered, they must be controlled and implicitly rectified, and the analysand's responses appropriately analyzed.

Introjective identification alludes to the interactional incorporation of contents, structures, and processes from another person. The study of such a mechanism includes not only the possibility that the recipient will reject the projective identification placed into him and repudiate its contents, but allows for processing and metabolizing the introjective contents along both distorted and nondistorted lines and for a wide range of reactions to them.

In the course of the therapeutic experience, both the patient and analyst project into and identify with the other participant, and interactionally attempt to effect projective and introjective identifications as well. The patient is continuously and unconsciously monitoring the state of the analyst, the extent to which he is capable of managing his internal conflicts, affects, fantasies, and objects, and the degree of his competence and effectiveness. He keeps track of the analyst's basic attitudes and interpretive abilities, and on this basis he effects a continuous, ever-changing series of introjective identifications with the analyst. Some of these identifications may be repeated and become structuralized and incorporated into the patient's self-representation, modifying his internal structures and objects, capacities for management, his intrapsychic conflicts, and the qualities of his ego functioning and basic adaptive strengths. Other identifications are more temporary and passing, although at times they may have significant momentary influence; all pathogenic introjective identifications and inappropriate uses of the analysand as a container for the analyst's pathology must eventually be identified, rectified, analyzed and worked through.

Interactionally, the patient experiences a variety of pathogenic and nonpathogenic projective identifications from the analyst. He may resist or contain them, refuting them or accepting them intrapsychically, elaborating upon them and utilizing them for constructive inner change or the reinforcement of his neurotic needs and structures, and for misalliance. The outcome represents an interactional amalgam and generally depends on the nature of the projective identification, the prevailing qualities of the bipersonal field and analytic interaction, and the inner state of the patient. Positively-toned introjective identifications with the analyst lead to a general strengthening of the personality and ego of the analysand, and reinforce his more positive functioning; by contrast, negative introjective identifications are disruptive in a variety of ways for the analysand, and generally disturb the therapeutic alliance and work. It is well to remember, however, that in addition to the positive projective identifications that are interactionally implicit in the analyst's valid interpretations and management of the framework, mildly pathological projective identifications may have salutary effects— in that they may mobilize the patient's adaptive resources and provide the analyst with information regarding his inner pathology. However, such benefit always accrues in the context of some disturbing qualities.

Generating Roles, Creating Images, or Evoking Reactions. There are a variety of interactional pressures from both the patient and analyst that may operate through projective and introjective identifications, but also rely on other interactional mechanisms that are more directly behavioral, though filled with unconscious meaning.

Without attempting a full metapsychological conception of these processes, we may note that either member of the dyad may endeavor to evoke behavioral responses or subjective reactions, or try to have the other participant accept or suffer with a particular self-image or conform to a particular image or role. There may be direct or indirect efforts at seduction, harm, inappropriate gratification, isolation, generation of affects such as anxiety and guilt, and the like. These interactional pressures are communicated directly and indirectly, and are implicit in the behaviors and verbalizations of either participant.

Patients will attempt to develop these images or responses from the analyst through conscious and unconscious misinterpretations of his interventions or management of the framework, and through specific forms of resistance; they may also develop acute regressive crises or stalemates, become involved in efforts at living out, or attempt to be overcompliant. The analyst, too, directly and indirectly, communicates expectations of the analysand that may include inappropriate behaviors, roles, affects, and the like. These pathological interactions may generate sectors of misalliance and disturb the therapeutic qualities of the bipersonal field. They also merit first-order analytic rectification and exploration, since they usually interfere with or preclude analytic work in the more verbal-fantasized sphere.

Among the most important of these interactional efforts is the attempt by either participant to evoke a proxy response in his counterpart. These are direct or indirect endeavors to evoke in the other party—the object—adaptive ego and superego responses, management capacities, instinctual-drive expressions and the like, that for some reason are unavailable to the subject for the moment. They may include efforts to have the object experience a particular type of mood, disrupted ego functioning, or instinctual wish that the subject either fears to experience or attempts to disown. While such interactional efforts are common within the analysand and may constitute for him appropriate as well as inappropriate interactional efforts, these mechanisms are also utilized by the analyst and are, for him, as a rule, inappropriate to the analytic setting.

These efforts may have defensive functions, but also a wide range of adaptive and maladative purposes. While they have a core symbiotic quality, they may be utilized by all types of patients and analysts, from those with primitive character structures to those who are relatively mature and intact. These evocations may entail a blurring of self-object boundaries, although they can also occur in the presence of clear-cut self-object differentiation. Only their pervasive or strikingly pathological use would suggest psychopathology more severe than that seen in neurotics. Evocation of proxies may be part of a regressive movement within the patient, but they may also aid his growth and development, or provide him with an opportunity to introject from the analyst adaptive ego and superego functions, including the adequate management of instinctual drive-related fantasies.

Interactionally, the analyst has a wide range of possible responses to the patient's efforts to evoke some type of proxy within him. As with projective identifications, he may become aware of these efforts and use them to understand and interpret to the patient, or he may respond in a countertransference-dominated manner that leads him to unconscious participation—creating a sector of misalliance. It is important that the analyst not unconsciously serve as a proxy for the patient at times of acute anxiety and conflict, and that he interpret such efforts to the anlysand so that he may develop his own adaptive capacities. These endeavors are to be distinguished from the analyst's basic stance and hold which offers a fundamental security to the patient rather than serving as a substitute proxy; clearly, there is overlap between the two.

Technically, the analyst should allow these efforts by the analysand to evoke proxies, role responses, self-images, and behaviors to reach a full but controlled level of intensity, but he must, as far as possible, avoid their gratification and any direct participation. His responses should be confined to "signal reactions" and to the necessary interventions. Momentary periods of participation in such misalliance-based interactions should be handled by the rectification of the analyst's involvement, and a full interpretation of the experience with the analysand.

The Interactional and Communicative Qualities of the Bipersonal Field

Having established some basic interactional mechanisms and processes, let us now examine on another level some of the characteristics of this field. Viewing the bipersonal field as a fluctuating and shared creation of the patient and analyst, we may briefly consider some of its communicative properties. These may be located within the patient, the analyst, or the field, and constitute all of the communicative qualities and processes that they share through their interaction. Turning to this aspect, we may first identify the *interface* of the interaction between the patient and the analyst. This is an ever-changing hypothetical surface or line which is determined by, and in turn determines, the nature and implications of the respective communications of the patient and analyst and receives continuous inputs, in varying proportions, from each.

1. Among the most important properties of the interface is its location, which may be relatively fixed or tend to fluctuate between the two polarities of the bipersonal field. Characteristically, the interface should be close to the patient and have a locus that is concentrated upon his psychopathology. Among the many factors that determine the location of the interface are the communicative powers of each participant and especially of their psychopathology, and the extent to which one or the other member of the dyad dominates the interaction and determines its properties. This locus is also determined by the framework, the patient's associations, and the analyst's interventions. Whether and to what extent the interface is fixed or mobile is related to the openness and variability of the avenues of communication, the extent to which the analytic relationship is fixed and deadlocked, the degree to which the analyst tends to place his own pathology into the field and to draw the interface toward his side of the polarity, and the degree to which outside influences are permitted to affect the location.

2. The interface has a variety of possible shapes and qualities; it is open to influence and modification by either participant and, through them, by outside influences. It may be predominantly verbal, action-oriented, or pervaded with affects and symptoms. It may be sharp or soft, compatible or incompatible, permeable or impermeable.

3. The interface of the analytic interaction has powerful effects on the intrapsychic state of both participants, and on their perception of themselves and each other. Each responds consciously and unconsciously to the efforts of his counterpart to shape and mold the interface, determine

its manifest and latent content, and its other properties. Their respective efforts and reactions to these pressures reflect important dimensions of neurotic and nonneurotic functioning in each member of the dyad. In all, a careful study of the interactional interface provides data about the special characteristics of the bipersonal field created by a given patient and analyst, as well as about their inner world and the interactional mechanisms used by each.

4. In addition to the attributes of the interface, we may conceptualize the communicative properties of the bipersonal field itself. Here too there are many dimensions, of which I will note the following: there may be a relatively open flow of conscious and unconscious communications—contents, affects, unconscious fantasies, and the like—or a general impairment in this flow (with contributions, it is to be remembered, from both participants). There may be split-off sectors—bastions—of the bipersonal field under repression or in a state of denial, created by sectors of misalliance so that certain aspects of the interaction and intrapsychic state of either or both participants is, through collusion, disregarded, or relatively closed off to recognition or conscious influence.

The unconscious motivations related to the communicative aspects of the field may have to do with mutual inappropriate gratifications on the one hand, or valid efforts toward cure on the other. In general, the main communicative qualities of the field may be classified as oriented toward verbal communication related to cognitive unconscious fantasies or, by contrast, action-oriented communications in which living out, the evocation of roles and proxies, and projective and introjective identifications predominate. While these may intermix, we may as a rule characterize the communicative qualities of the bipersonal field as predominantly one or the other.

5. In addition to these communicative aspects developed through the interaction between the patient and analyst, we may briefly characterize certain communicative properties within the patient and analyst. For the former, it is possible to consider the openness of his free associations, the extent of his resistances, the use of silences, and the misuse of associating for inappropriate gratifications. In addition, the motivations for his communications may be directed either toward cure or toward resistance and inappropriate gratification—for example toward the harm, seduction, or frustration of the analyst. Still another important communicative line may be best termed the *me/not me interface* of the patient's associations. All communications from the analysand allude on some level both to himself and to his objects, especially the analyst, regardless of the manifest content. This interface is expecially relevant to the analyst's task of sorting out the patient's introjections of the analyst. Finally, there is the extent to which the analysand consciously and unconsciously experiences his associations as pertaining to himself rather than to others. This depends partly on the "closeness" (relatively undisguised) or "distance" (relatively disguised) of the manifest expressions of derivatives of unconscious fantasies and introjects (Langs 1973). These may be vehemently disowned by the patient, or readily accepted by him as part of his self-image and experience. Both the analyst's subjective assessment of such communications and his actual influence on them must be recognized and investigated.

There appear to be two basic kinds of communicative styles or spaces available for the analysand. One involves verbal communication related to affectively toned derivatives of unconscious fantasies, memories, and introjects; this type of communicative space is the basis for the classical psychoanalytic conception of communication, resistance, and interpretation in the analytic situation. The second style or space is basically interactional and centers upon the evocation of roles and proxies, the use of interactional mechanisms, the development of interactional resistances, and the presence of interactional defenses. Certain aspects of this communicative space have been carefully studied by the Kleinian psychoanalysts, although the influence of external realities and the recognition of this type of communication as a basic form within the analytic relationship has not been especially developed. Technically, it is important to recognize the preponderant properties of the communicative space within which the patient expresses himself so that the analyst's interventions are in keeping with the prevailing mode. Successful analytic insight and structural change may occur through analytic work in either space.

Finally, one may think of the patient's mode of communication in the verbal-fantasy sphere as containing or failing to contain identifiable and analyzable derivatives. Patients may communicate many derivatives of unconscious fantasies and introjects without presenting the organizing adaptive context. They may present the adaptive context and communicate only their direct or surface responses without conveying meaningful unconscious derivatives. They may present a variety of derivatives and, in passing, convey the adaptive context; or they may communicate without either an identifiable adaptive context or a meaningful set of derivatives. When these communicative dimensions and styles are under the influence of the analyst, they are best viewed as qualities of the bipersonal field. When the analyst is able to separate himself from them and interpret their use to the analysand—a type of intervention that must precede in most instances the therapeutic work with analyzable contents—these styles are essentially determined by the unconscious needs and fantasies (as well as other factors) within the analysand.

Because of the differences in his role and functions, we need a different classification of the communicative properties of the analyst. This study may be initiated by identifying the source of his most frequent interventions: silences, confrontations, questions, interpretations, and reconstructions. We may consider next the extent to which he offers valid interventions, the qualities of his management of the framework, and the frequency and nature of his errors. The analyst's erroneous interventions may primarily communicate his own pathological intrapsychic fantasies and introjects, and be largely verbal-fantasy communications. As a rule, however, because an erroneous intervention is an action, there will always be present elements of living out, inappropriate efforts to evoke roles and proxies, and the use of pathological projective identifications. The analyst's more direct behaviors may show a preference for the utilization of living out and interactional mechanisms, and his own particular preference for a particular type of communicative space and style. As a rule, this bias will have a significant influence on the analysand's communicative mechanisms. Since these are aspects of the analytic interaction that have received only minimal consideration in this literature to date, I will not pursue them further here; they point to important avenues of future clinical research.

Distance and Closeness
Between Patient and Analyst

Effective analytic work depends upon the maintenance of optimal distance between the two participants—a distance that is a property of their interaction within the bipersonal field. There are continuous pressures within both participants to widen or reduce this distance, and these needs are communicated interactionally in a variety of ways.

The concept of *distance* embraces the emotional or affective relatedness between patient and analyst, the extent to which they are working together, and the degree to which they are meaningfully communicating and in touch, or to which each is attempting to invoke barriers, conflict, and disruptions in their relationship. Underlying these more surface components are deeper mechanisms such as the extent of mutual identification, the respective fluidity of ego boundaries and the capacity to restore these boundaries when interrupted, the extent to which projections and projective identifications are in effect, the openness of introjective identifications and containing functions, and the unconscious image that one participant has of the other. These complex factors are influenced, in turn, by the patient's and analyst's unconscious fantasies, introjects, and conflicts on the one hand, and ego functions and capacities to relate on the other.

Optimal distance may be defined as a point where close, meaningful communication has been effected without undue defensiveness and where communication is open, in terms both of the patient's expression of derivatives of unconscious fantasies and of his interactional needs with the analyst, and the analyst's responsive openness to contain, experience, metabolize, and interpret. Important here are the analyst's empathic, identificatory, and cognitive capacities, which neither are maintained too intensely (e.g., fixed or too intense identifications with the analysand) nor are too defended (e.g., failures in empathy, defenses against temporary identification, and the like).

Unconscious needs related to neurotic defenses and gratifications may lead either participant to create distance or to move especially close. Such efforts by the analysand can be experienced subjectively by the analyst, and detected and analyzed from the patient's verbal and nonverbal communications; the underlying basis for the impairments involved must be resolved.

In general, when the patient is too distant or too close, interpretations are not experienced primarily in terms of their intended meanings, but will have other communicative influences, unless they are directed at the interactional problem itself. Under such conditions, the analyst's interventions will tend either to further increase the patient's distance from him or prompt a shift toward excessive closeness; they will not lead to cognitive insight. Distance maintained by the patient implies defensiveness, resistance, and some degree of negation of the relationship. Such remoteness often goes hand in hand with intrapsychic defenses and a need to be removed from one's own inner fantasy life.

Undue closeness, on the other hand, may be related to the failure of interactional or intrapsychic defenses, acute regressions, intensifed intrapsychic conflicts, heightening of instinctual-drive needs, and difficulties in maintaining self-object boundaries. As a rule, it is expressed through inappropriately blatant communications of seductive or incorporative needs. Such closeness or efforts toward fusion may also represent the expression of hostile and destructive wishes, and thereby have an attacking or penetrating quality, and include endeavors to frighten off the analyst or to seduce and draw him inappropriately closer.

Technically, interpretations related to disturbances in this sphere take precedence over work with the content of the patient's communications, since such disturbances tend to interfere with interpretive work in the cognitive sphere. In addition, this sphere is pertinent to the therapeutic alliance, since an optimal alliance relies on the maintenance of an ideal degree of distance and closeness. Disturbances are, of course, inevitable, and their resolution provides important insights for the analysand who struggles with comparable problems within himself and in his outside relationships.

Interactional Realities

Within the bipersonal field are the realities of how the analyst functions. Who he is, his unconscious intentions, and the implicit communications in his interventions are of considerable importance. They convey the nature of his intrapsychic balances and capacity to manage his inner state. These interactional realities are often expressed nonverbally or inferred, latent within the manifest content or intentions of the analyst's communications, and they have a major adaptive effect upon the patient, who consistently monitors, perceives, and incorporates these aspects of the analyst's behaviors. In addition to what they reveal about the analyst, they are an essential means through which the patient may come to distinguish, on both surface and deeply unconscious levels, the analyst from past pathogenic figures, and the analytic interaction from past pathogenic interactions.

These interactional realities have, in effect, first-order meanings for the patient, and they take precedence over the analyst's consciously intended behaviors and verbal communications, which they negate unless in consonance with them. The tone, timing, unconscious meanings, and projective qualities of the analyst's verbal interpretations, then, have a significant influence on the analysand. Discrepancies between the analyst's manifest intentions and his unconscious communications will evoke negative images of him as hypocritical and confused, and disruptive unconscious communications generate negative introjective identifications and tend to confirm the patient's past and present pathological inner and outer realities.

Interactional Resistances

We turn now to a selected group of clinically important properties of the bipersonal field—condensations of the efforts of the patient and the analyst. Turning first to *interactional resistances*, we may note that in addition to their basic intrapsychic defensive and gratifying aspects, all resistances have important adaptive and interactional aspects, and at times may best be viewed as products of the bipersonal field. Resistances, as we know, are expressions within the analytic relationship of the patient's intrapsychic defense as they are reflected in his efforts to interfere with the progress of the analytic work. As a rule, they are provoked by the appearance of derivatives of anxiety-arousing unconscious fantasies, memories, and introjects evoked by a specific adaptive context. The analysis of the intrapsychic component of a resistance relies on the recognition of that essential adaptive context, and a full exploration of the related intrapsychic conflicts and unconscious meanings of the resistance itself.

In the context of this analytic work, we may identify first of all the interactional aspects of the evaluation of the analysand's resistances: the assessment by the analyst that a specific behavior or communication from the patient essentially constitutes a resistance. This determination is based on a variety of interactional factors, including the analyst's subjective clinical judgment, the range of his inner feelings and ideas, and his perceptions of the patient. In conceptualizing the patient's communications as primarily in the service of resistance, the analyst is judging the analysand as defensive and interfering. Interactionally, there are dangers of denial, repression, projection, and misunderstanding by the analyst; careful use of the validating process is essential. The subjective elements in this assessment have been largely overlooked in this literature.

The concept that the patient is resisting usually implies opposition to the analyst. It may therefore be utilized inappropriately to confront the patient in a manner that actually represents an unconscious attack. Thus, an incorrect assessment that the patient is in a state of resistance and an intervention offered on such a basis may be part of interactional efforts by the analyst to pathologically projectively identify into and evoke inappropriate responses within the patient. The relevant contents are often related to the narcissistic and aggressive needs of the analyst. Both the assessment and interpretation of resistances therefore have important interactional components.

In a second area, resistance mechanisms may afford unconscious interactional gratifications and protections to the patient—and analyst. A patient's defenses may be mobilized to master not only intrapsychic anxieties, but also interpersonal anxieties. A resistance may thwart or constitute an attack upon the analyst, provoke him to seductive behaviors, undermine his self-image, or create distance and barriers between him and the patient. These experiences may be unconsciously disturbing or inappropriately gratifying to the analyst, who may conduct himself in a way that unconsciously encourages their expression or as a therapeutic alternative modifies their presence through valid interpretations. When the analyst, through inappropriate communications on any level, prompts or reinforces the analysand's resistances, these may be explicitly termed *interactional resistances*.

A third interactional aspect occurs when the patient uses the manifest and latent content of his resistance and its actual presence projectively, to put into the analyst aspects of his own inner defenses and disturbed state, or when he introjects projective identifications from the analyst with strong defensive elements. In these instances, the analysand's resistance gratifies the unconscious fantasies and interactional needs of the analyst. The patient, for instance, may accept the analyst's wish for the analysand to remain sick, not to communicate in certain areas, or to disrupt the unfolding of the treatment; or he may introjectively identify with those aspects of the analyst that place into the patient defenses and contents designed to intensify the resistances of the analysand. These interactions then constitute sectors of misalliance in which the patient has complied with the unconsciously perceived and incorporated wishes from the analyst for defense and resistance; they too represent interactional resistances.

Technically, the analysis of any apparent resistance calls first for the use of the validating process to confirm that a given behavior or communication is indeed primarily an expression of resistance; and second, a full analysis of its intrapsychic and interactional determinants, including the contributions of the analyst. Here, the self-analytic rectification of the analyst's misconception or actual reinforcement of the resistance must take precedence, since it is the foundation for verbal-interpretive analytic work; so long as the unconscious collusion persists, the resistance will not be properly interpreted or analytically modified.

Interactional Symptoms

The concept of the bipersonal field directs the analysis of the patient's symptoms not only toward his intrapsychic conflicts and pathological introjects, but toward the interactional components that unconsciously contribute to the appearance of a symptomatic disturbance within the analysand. Basic analytic investigations have indicated that a symptom is derived from an unconscious conflict and from pathological fantasies and introjects that are handled by the ego in the face of failing defenses through a compromise formation that takes into account all of the intrapsychic agencies of the patient's mind and external reality as well. However, closer scrutiny of the analytic interaction indicates that on a number of levels there are additional interactional components to symptom formation within the analysand—both genetically and in the present.

First, a symptom always conveys unconscious meanings to the analyst—it has a communicative function. An hysterical paralysis, for example, could communicate defenses against the wish to be held by the analyst, an unconscious perception of the analyst's ineptness, or a defense against the perception of his destructiveness toward the patient. It may therefore be based on both unconscious fantasy and unconscious perception; processes in both spheres contribute to the ultimate compromise formation.

Secondly, the analysand's symptoms may be partly based on his incorporation of the analyst's unconscious pathological needs and fantasies. A symptom may there-fore represent an introjective identification with the analyst's general wishes that the patient be sick and helpless or that he have difficulty managing his intrapsy-chic fantasies. In addition, it may represent the introjec-tion of specific unconscious fantasies and introjects that have been verbally or nonverbally communicated to or projected into the patient.

In a well-run analytic experience, we would expect that the main contributions to a symptom in the analysand would derive from his intrapsychic conflicts and interac-tional needs. We would further expect most symptoms to occur within the analysand. However, we must be prepared to find that at times a symptom experienced by the patient has significant determinants in the uncon-scious fantasies and conflicts of the analyst, and in his interactional projective identifications into the patient. At times, too, a countertransference symptom within the analyst will have essential determinants derived from the patient and the interaction with him—in addition to those that derive from within the analyst himself.

These symptoms of the bipersonal field may be termed *interactional symptoms;* as a rule, the presence of any symptom in either member of the dyad calls for a careful scrutiny of its unconscious structure and the search for contributions from both participants. Here, too, rectification of the analyst's actual contributions to the patient's symptoms, as conveyed through unconscious communications or interactional mechanisms, is a prerequisite for interpreta-tion and resolution of the disturbance through insight. It seems likely that many symptoms that appear during the course of an analysis that previously have been viewed as components of the transference neurosis are, with more careful scrutiny, actually derived from the analytic interaction, and that they contain important transference and nontransference components. A discussion of the relevance of these observations to the subject of symptom formation in general, while a promising avenue of study, is beyond the scope of this discussion.

Interactional Syndromes

The symptoms in the analysand, and at times in the analyst, as derived from both intrapsychic and interactional factors, may coalesce into a syndrome of the bipersonal field that may be termed an *interactional syndrome*—an interactional neurosis, psychosis, or borderline cluster of symptoms. Thus, we should reserve the term *transference neurosis* or *syndrome* for the concentration of those symptoms in the analysand that derive essentially from his unconscious conflicts and fantasies about the analyst, and use the term *interactional neurosis* or *syndrome* when there are significant contributions from the unconscious perceptions and introjects of the analyst's pathology. Inappropriate disturbances in the analytic relationship often crystallize in symptom formation and characterological difficulties within either or both of the participants in the analytic situation, thereby creating syndromes of the bipersonal field. The interactional syndrome is therefore a compromise formation that includes components from the analytic interaction as well as bilateral intrapsychic aspects and added contributions from external reality.

It is primarily when the analyst is under the influence of extended, unresolved countertransference problems which prompt inappropriate communications to the analysand and repeated pathological efforts at projective identification, that an extensive interactional syndrome will emerge. Most often, interactional symptoms are the rule. These interactional constellations, however, call for extensive self-analytic work within the analyst so that his involvement in the patient's illness can be rectified, creating the conditions for sound analytic work regarding the patient's contributions to his own illness.

Interactional Insight and Interpretations

Within the bipersonal field, insight may be defined as the analytic resolution of a shared blind spot or failure to comprehend, and the positive creation of meaningful understanding. While insight may develop in either the patient or analyst without a significant interactional component, and may derive largely from a modification of the patient's intrapsychic defenses and resultant communications, most often this process reflects a modification of interactional, shared defenses and the emergence of new interactional communications as well. Frequently, there are initial sectors of misalliance that create failures in understanding and contain components of both transference and countertransference. In addition to the resolution of such sectors, positive interactional inputs from both participants, including the adaptive use of interactional mechanisms, contribute to the development of comprehension.

Unconsciously, the patient interactionally contributes to virtually all of the analyst's understanding and failure to understand. If he projectively identifies into the analyst good parts of himself or unconsciously generates a benign and helpful image of the analyst, he will unconsciously communicate and place into the analyst meaningful verbal and interactional derivatives. The analyst will in turn be in a postion to comprehend and interpret to the patient. If, on the other hand, the patient wishes to projectively identify into the analyst good, bad, or destructive parts of himself as well as aspects of his inner disturbances in a form designed to confuse the analyst and disrupt his functioning, he may effect periods during which understanding and insight do not occur. Further, in certain mutually sensitive areas, the patient and analyst may develop a sector of misalliance in which a dimension of the patient's intrapsychic conflicts and pathological unconscious fantasies is sealed off from comprehension and maintained for mutual inappropriate gratification and defense. Thus, the analyst's construction of an interpretation is not only the outcome of a complex set of his own internal processes, but evolves out of the unconscious interaction between himself and the patient. Moments of insight tend to occur at a point in the analytic interaction at which the respective unconscious forces within the patient and analyst move toward a more adaptive resolution of their interactional syndrome and the components derived intrapsychically from each participant.

Interactional Symptom Resolution

Symptom alleviation within the patient may reflect valid, adaptive structural changes derived from insight, conflict resolution, positive introjective identifications, and a resolution of an interactional neurosis; it may therefore be based on intrapsychic and interactional factors. At times, however, symptom relief may stem maladaptively from a sector of therapeutic misalliance which reinforces the patient's intrapsychic defenses or momentarily gratifies his neurotic inner needs. Rather than a *transference* or *countertransference cure*, the interactional components of noninsightful symptom relief appear best termed a *misalliance cure* to indicate the interactional contributions of both transference and countertransference components.

The distinction between basically adaptive intrapsychic or interactional symptom resolution and that which is primarily maladaptive depends on an extensive use of the validating process and, especially, a review of the antecedents of symptom relief. In addition, the analyst's subsequent subjective reactions and the patient's associations will reveal in derivative form the underlying basis for the symptom modification.

An important form of *misalliance cure* is the *framework* or *boundary cure*, which occurs when the patient or analyst, with or without the cooperation of the other participant, effects an unneeded modification in the frame with consequent symptom relief based on unilaterally gained or shared inappropriate gratifications or defensive reinforcements. As a rule, these efforts have an interactional basis and may also be viewed as a form of interactional resistance.

In general, most misalliance cures tend to be temporary and break down either with careful analytic rectification and exploration of the underlying factors or through the failure of one of the participants to maintain the shared pathology involved. It is feasible, however, for this type of symptom alleviation to be structuralized and to take on adaptive value, although by and large this solidification includes reliance on the use of pathological defenses and interactions. It is this type of symptom relief that predominates in noninsightful, nonanalytic treatment and in poorly managed anlyses and psychotherapies.

Technical Considerations of
the Bipersonal Field

We have now come to recognize that there are two spheres of the analyst's activity. The first is based on the patient's verbal associations and the derivatives of his unconscious fantasies, memories, and introjects contained therein, with lesser contributions from more apparent interactional components. This is essentially the sphere of analytic work that, with an emphasis on transference, has been the main focus of the classical psychoanalyst. The second area of analytic activity involves the analysis of the unconscious fantasies, memories, introjects, and mechanisms that are pertinent to and expressed in the patient's interaction with the analyst. It is this area that, as we have seen, has largely preoccupied the Kleinian psychoanalysts who, however, have focused almost exclusively on the projective and introjective identificatory mechanisms involved, with a relative exclusion of other interactional components, especially neglecting the realities that prompt such interactional efforts. Analytic work within both spheres and in keeping with the patient's predominant preference is crucial to ultimate therapeutic outcome.

There are many complex technical issues related to the interactional dimension. Among the most vexing is the problem of when to withhold interpretations and to make use of management of the frame because the patient's needs involve difficulties that call for a securing of the basic analytic hold rather a verbal intervention, and when to interpret components of the interaction rather than deal primarily with verbalized derivatives. In brief, as I have indicated, much of this depends on the patient's primary mode of expression and the type of analytic space within which he prefers to convey the derivatives of his inner disturbances—the realm within which he communicates analyzable derivatives. In addition, a basic technical precept indicates that the analyst must deal with interactional mechanisms and processes before those related to verbalized derivatives, since the actuality of the former takes precedence for the analysand over the influence of his fantasies, although clearly both intermix.

When the patient is interactionally mobilized, his verbal associations will most meaningfully relate to his interactional efforts, and interpretations in other areas will not be adaptively pertinent and, generally, will remain unconfirmed. Any important subjective interactional experience within the analyst, as well as any period during which he is unable to formulate the patient's associations around fantasy-based derivatives, calls for a scrutiny of the interaction and and for the possibility of interpretations or managements in this area. This sphere may contain important expressions of unconscious fantasies and introjects, as well as defenses that merit intervention. In addition, there is the unique characteristic of interactional processes and actualities that the analyst may be significantly contributing to the nature of the interaction, including its pathological aspects. It is here that the important additional step of rectifying his pathological contribution precedes the interpretive resolution of the relevant pathology within the patient. Consistent use of the validating process is essential to such work.

Concluding Comments

In bringing this overview and synthesis to a close, I want to reestablish a perspective, since those analysts who have focused on the patient-analyst interaction have often been criticized for disregarding the central role of reconstructions and interpretations in the basic psychoanalytic process. I have tried repeatedly to make clear my belief that the main factors of cure derive from basically interwoven facets of the analyst's stance and communications, and his actualities, interactions, and verbalizations. The analyst cannot offer an effective reconstruction or interpretation in the absence of a sound relationship with the patient; nor can he silently and implicitly be a model for constructive identifications without the crucial ability to maintain the framework and offer well-timed reconstructions and interpretations. Further, he cannot effectively deal with interactional processes and mechanisms without understanding the patient's verbal communications, interpret unconscious fantasies without a sound conception of the space through which the analytic interaction proceeds.

Both interpretation and relationship are essential for cure. It is not a matter of which one takes precedence, but how each complements and reinforces the other, and which aspect will predominate for a given patient-analyst pairing, from moment to moment in the analytic work. The complete analyst is a feeling human being, an effective manager of the framework, and a capable interpreter. Extending this model to the analytic interaction, we must recognize that a full comprehension is feasible only when the intrapsychic and interactional facets are both taken into account.

Looking back over this synthesis, I am reminded again of the virtual impossibility for the analyst to maintain constant mastery over the incredibly complex relationship between himself and the analysand. Similarly, any attempt to explore and define the multiple components of this relationship and interaction is bound to falter in places, and to leave a sense of dissatisfaction at some junctures.

There are inevitable omissions, and many discussions will evoke controversy and debate; only a certain—hopefully significant—portion can prove illuminating to the point of full consideration and of truly durable substance.

However, if this volume does nothing more than prompt an intensive reexamination of the analytic interaction, I will consider myself to have been sufficiently successful in the goals I set. If it has crystallized some important new insights, I am more than satisfied. Above all, I hope that I have demonstrated that psychoanalysis is by far the single most viable means of comprehending the therapeutic relationship, and that it offers a set of revisable theoretical and clinical constructs that are neither so rigidly set as to be fossilized, nor so clearly understood that they no longer generate curiosity, scientific and clinical questioning and challenge, excitement for the potential investigator, and hope for a more effective means of cure for the patient. With this overview and synthesis completed, it seems now that we should return to the clinical setting for renewed investigation designed to move us closer to the resolution of the important perplexing and provocative issues that we have been considering here. We know a great deal and we have much to learn.

References

Freud, S. (1923). Remarks on the theory and practice of dream-interpretation. *Standard Edition* 19:109-121.

Langs, R. (1973). *The Technique of Psychoanalytic Psychotherapy, Vol. I.* New York: Jason Aronson.

——— (1974). *The Technique of Psychoanalytic Psychotherapy, Vol. II.* New York: Jason Aronson.

——— (1975a). Therapeutic misalliances. *International Journal of Psychoanalytic Psychotherapy* 4:77-105.

——— (1975b). The therapeutic relationship and deviations in technique. *International Journal of Psychoanalytic Psychotherapy* 4:106-141.

——— (1975c). The patient's unconscious perception of the therapist's errors. In *Tactics and Techniques in Psychoanalytic Psychotherapy, Vol. II: Countertransference*, ed. Peter L. Giovacchini. New York: Jason Aronson.

——— (1976a). *The Bipersonal Field.* New York: Jason Aronson.

——— (1976b). *The Therapeutic Interaction.* 2 vols. New York: Jason Aronson.

Index

as source of countertransference reactions, 114
and transference, 78-80
and transference-based projections, 64-68
psychoanalysis, compared with psychotherapy and validating process, 4-11
psychoanalytic situation, defined, 4-6
psychotherapeutic situation, defined, 4-6
psychotherapy, compared with psychoanalysis and validating process, 4-11

reactions, evoking of, as basic interactional component of analytic relationship, 171-174
reactive countertransference responses, 111-112
See also countertransference
reactive noncountertransference, 133
See also noncountertransference
reactive transference
active, 59-60
passive, 60
in patient's relationship to analyst, 54-61
See also transference
realities
current, in matrix nontransference, 100
interactional, 182-183
nature of, and framework, 28
real relationship, 98, 106
receptive functioning, and forms of noncountertransference expression, 133-134
rectification, of modified frame, 33
regression, bilateral therapeutic, 9, 10
resistance
interactional, 183-186
and reactive transference, 59
transference-based creation of, 53
response, in analytic situation, 12-13, 16
analyst's subjective and intuitive, 15, 16
roles, generating of, as basic interactional component of analytic relationship, 171-174

role sensitivity, and forms of noncountertransference expression, 133-134

safeguards, and frame, 36
"screen," projective, and frame, 35-36
security, and frame, 28, 34, 54
self-analysis, analyst's, 125
See also misalliance, therapeutic
signal experiences, 138
signal reactions, 174
silence, analyst's, 15, 16
symptoms
as form of transference expression, 71, 85
interactional, 186-188
resolution of, 190-191
syndromes, interactional, 188-189

termination, sudden premature, 160, 163
therapeutic alliance
definition of, 149
impairments in, in interactional processes, 159-166
bilateral, misalliances, 163-166
unilateral disturbances derived primarily from analyst, 163
unilateral disturbances derived primarily from patient, 160-162
in interactional processes, 147-149
sources of, in interactional processes, 149-156
transference as a motive force in, 53
time, of analytic session as frame, 29, 37
transference
active reactive, 59-60
component, in patient's relationship to analyst, 52-54
definition of, 52, 73
expression, forms of, 72-85
acting or living out, 74-76
belief, intention, distorted perception, delusion, and hallucination, 81-85
as conscious fantasy, 72-74
interaction with analyst, 76-81
predominant function of, in patient's relationship to analyst, 88-90